INNER POWER

INNER POWER

Secrets from Tibet and the Orient

By Christopher S. Kilham

Japan Publications, Inc.

Published by JAPAN PUBLICATIONS, INC., Tokyo and New York

Distributors:
UNITED STATES: *Kodansha International/USA, Ltd., through Harper & Row, Publishers, Inc., 10 East 53rd Street, New York, N. Y. 10022.* SOUTH AMERICA: *Harper & Row, Publishers, Inc., International Department.* CANADA: *Fitzhenry & Whiteside Ltd., 150 Lesmill Road, Don Mills, Ontario, M3B 2T6.* MEXICO AND CENTRAL AMERICA: *HARLA S. A. de C. V., Apartado 30–546, Mexico 4 D. F.* BRITISH ISLES: *Premier Book Marketing Ltd., 1 Gower Street, London WC1E 6HA.* EUROPEAN CONTINENT: *European Book Service PBD, Strijkviertel 63, 3454 PK de Meern, The Netherlands.* AUSTRALIA AND NEW ZEALAND: *Bookwise International, 1 Jeanes Street, Beverley, South Australia 5009.* THE FAR EAST AND JAPAN: *Japan Publications Trading Co., Ltd., 1–2–1, Sarugaku-cho, Chiyoda-ku, Tokyo 101.*

First edition: October 1988

LCCC No. 88–080452
ISBN 0–87040–689–2

Printed in U.S.A.

Turiya

I'm cruising through the Milky Way
My headlights burning bright
Leaving tracks across the galaxy
And stardust in the night.
I'm shooting through a bubbling sea
Of stars and space and time
And roaring 'round the Universe
With nothing on my mind.

My craft throws flames and jet spray
Bursting flashes in the sky
Washing white the soundless borders
Of great floating nebulae.
And I feel an awesome power
And hear great melodic strains
As I bank against the farthest light
And head back home again.

Oh! to trip the light fantastic
Past the charted realms of man
Is to drink the draughts of ecstasy
And see a greater Plan
Which guides the hand of destiny,
Illuminates the skies,
Gives thrust to our trajectory,
And validates our lives.

FELIX BLISS

Contents

Foreword, 11

Acknowledgments, 13

1. Power, 15

2. The Cultivation of Power, 19

3. The Human Energy System, 27

   The Chakra System, 28
   Ida, Pingala, Sushumna, 30
   The First Chakra, Muladhara, 30
   The Second Chakra, Svadhistana, 30
   The Third Chakra, Manipura, 31
   The Fourth Chakra, Anahata, 31
   The Fifth Chakra, Visuddha, 32
   The Sixth Chakra, Ajna, 32
   The Seventh Chakra, Sahasrara, 32
   Kundalini, 33
   Meridians, 34
   The Aura, 35

4. Power of the Breath, 37

   The Breaths of Buddha Hands, 40
   Training Breathing, 41
   Open Lotus Breathing, 41
   Snake Breathing, 42
   Flying Crane Breathing, 43
   Ten Tibetan Breaths, 44
   The Aura Builder, 47
   The Invincible Breath, 49
   The Vibrational Breaths, 50
   The Sun in the Heart, 51
   Initiate's Breath, 52
   The Immortal Breath, 53
   The Shakti Breath, 54

8

5. Chuang Fu, 55

6. The Five Elements Exercises, 69

7. The Five Tibetans, 77

8. Kundalini Yoga, 87

    Spinal Twists, 90
    Siddhasan, 91
    Lotus Pose, 92
    Lotus Alternate Knee Breathing, 93
    Cat Stretch, 94
    Mahamudra, 95
    Reverse Seal, 96
    Yoga Mudra, 97
    Yoni Mudra, 98
    More on Kundalini, 99

9. Power Generators, 101

    Solar Plexus Charging, 102
    Energy Polarization, 103
    Chi Development Method, 104

10. Siva's High Magic—The Invocation of the Shadow, 107

11. Cosmic Meditation, 111

    Kundalini Yoga Meditation, 113
    Nad Yoga: Sound Current Meditation, 114
    Silver Cord Meditation, 116
    Center of the Skull, 117

    Glossary, 119

    Index, 123

Foreword

As far as I am concerned, the world is a very strange place to live. It is mysterious, awesome, powerful, surprising, and delightful in a million ways. It is also dangerous; no one gets out alive.

Inner Power is about the cultivation of keen senses, a strong body, electrifying energy, a clear mind, and a very particular attitude about living in this world. It is a particular path, the sum total of one's travels in this life. *Inner Power* is a unique approach to developing the latent, potent forces within us.

Is one path ultimately more valid than another? One can spend an entire lifetime endeavoring to answer the question. The path of power is a way of developing the body, mind, and spirit, so that one may pursue the adventure of living to maximum advantage. This path is not for everyone. Human temperaments vary greatly, and what is right for one person is not necessarily suitable for another.

The world is not neat and tidy like a parcel of laundry, but is instead a churning sea of mystery and power. Since the dawn of humanity, people have embarked upon quests of all dimensions, by which they have explored the world, endeavoring to fathom its secrets. Some explorers set off to the jungles of South America, to the Himalayas, or out onto the open seas. Other explorers play in the fields of the body and the mind, attempting to unravel the secrets of the human being. Through various forms of yoga, martial arts, meditation, sacred dance, and even drugs, the body and mind have been explored for thousands of years, and still the secrets of the human being have not all been revealed. There is much to know.

The writing of this book is very much a part of my own exploration of the body-mind. In my own travels I have explored meditation, yoga, the martial arts, magic, and shamanism, and there is some of all these in the pages that follow. *Inner Power* is certainly not the definitive guide to all there is to know about the human being. Rather, it is like a collection of tools which comprise a modest workshop. With these tools one can build a personal practice which is useful for exploring this mysterious world.

The methods described in this book have been used and developed, in some cases, for thousands of years. In and of itself, this fact is not a guarantee of authenticity. But it is worth noting that these methods and techniques have proven useful for strengthening the body, purifying and vitalizing the human energy system, training the mind, and cultivating an indomitable spirit. Practitioners experience many of the same results when they use similar methods. However, if you practice any or all of these techniques, the results you obtain will be peculiar to your own body-mind system.

Proceeding along the path of power is not a frivolous endeavor. However, I believe that an overly serious attitude acts like a slow poison. If any elements of personality are universally useful, they are curiosity and a sense of humor. After all, we are in a very funny predicament. We are born into a world that we do not know, for reasons that we do not understand, and we are surrounded by people and things which frequently do not make sense. In the midst of this uncertainty, we attempt to figure out what is going on, while being bombarded by theories, rules, religions, and sciences, all of which change continually. Today's gods are tomorrow's myths.

This curious set of circumstances can represent a horribly depressing existential dilemma, or can be regarded as a unique opportunity to explore the world and develop oneself. For me, the latter option is more appealing. We really do not know what all of this life is about, but we are here, we are equipped with perceptual tools, and we are capable of learning. Right away it seems as though we have more going for ourselves than, say, rocks do.

In this book I have tried not to insult the reader with the unnecessary mumbo jumbo, vagaries, and exaggerated claims which typify much of the literature about self-development. I have, however, attempted to create a mood, a style, and a certain attitude with which to convey the nature of the methods and information found on these pages. It is my sincere wish that what is written here will be useful, and will help readers tread the path of self-fulfillment skillfully and with great success.

CHRISTOPHER S. KILHAM

Acknowledgments

I would like to express my appreciation and gratitude to the following individuals, whose wisdom, advice, energy, presence, or other attributes have in some way contributed to my own Body-Mind Synthesis, and therefore to the creation of this book: Rev. Victor F. Scalise, Herakhan Babaji, Swami Rudrananda, Maharishi Mahesh Yogi, J. Krishnamurti, Swami Satchitananda, Sri Chinmoy, Swami Satyeswarananda, Swami Muktananda, Swami Vedavyasananda, Yogiraj Vethathiri Maharishi, Lama Yeshe, Lama Zopa, Chogyam Trungpa, Ram Dass, Paramahansa Yogananda, Neem Karoli Baba, Rolling Thunder, Alex Anatolev, and Felix Bliss.

1. Power

What is power? It is the capacity to act, or to influence. Power may be physical, such as the ability to pick up a stone. It may be mental, such as the capacity to figure out a mathematical problem. Power may be political, social, psychic, financial, emotional, religious, or otherwise. There are no limits to the possibilities of power, no boundaries to its expression. Being powerful means having the capacity to act or influence in the world. Your capacity may be great or small; the choice is up to you. In the context of this book, power is a psycho-biological capacity, that is, a capacity of the body-mind. It is a natural potential which is only rarely fully developed. The important point is that it can be developed, deliberately and systematically.

Power is a strange thing. Some people seem to be naturally powerful. They act as they wish, and they influence as they choose. They achieve desired outcomes; in other words, they get what they want. For other people, living powerfully is not easy. They do not achieve desired outcomes, and thus often do not get what it is that they want. In thought, word, and deed, such people find themselves at the receiving end of circumstance, rather than in a position of control. What makes the difference? Family, upbringing, education, friends, and social conditions are certainly contributing factors. Yet people from all backgrounds are powerful. How and why this is so is something which cannot easily be explained. Among those who are powerful, however, there do seem to be two common factors. One is a belief in oneself. Most of the influential people I have met have had a fundamental belief in themselves. They believe that they can accomplish their goals, whatever those goals might be. Secondly, they persist. Nothing triumphs like persistence. Neither faith nor genius nor talent can match being persistent for obtaining results. Persistence often works when all else fails.

Not only are some people more powerful than others, but there is a prevalent fear of power itself, as though somehow power is innately evil. This notion is patently absurd. Power itself cannot be corrupt. People certainly can be corrupt. Individuals can use their influence to the detriment of other individuals and society at large. But power itself is not to be feared or shunned. Being powerful is being effective. There is a saying that "Power corrupts, and absolute power corrupts absolutely." It is a quaint saying, and a funny play on words. However, it is inaccurate.

There is no guarantee that a person will live in a kind, considerate, incorrupt manner. But is that any reason to condemn living powerfully? For every Hitler there is a Gandhi. For every sociopath there is a lover of humanity. What are we to do? Shall we outlaw being a powerful person? Shall we homogenize ourselves into a society of vacant-faced automatons? Or shall we deliberately pursue powerful, satisfying lives? To live in a healthful, ecological, kind, positive manner is a great challenge of being a human being. I know of no way to get around that challenge. Just live up to it, that is all. And do it with power.

Power also invokes superstition. Powerful people are often capable of doing what others cannot. Thus they are often considered to be supernatural, divine, magical, or otherwise endowed with abilities beyond normal human potential. What a sham this is. We have yet to know the full potential of a human being. But there is no doubt that it is more vast than the galaxies, more fantastic than our wildest dreams, more spectacular than anything we have ever imagined. Some people have walked on water, walked on fire, pulled objects out of thin air, levitated, accurately predicted the future, read the minds of others, healed diseases by thought alone, and performed other wondrous feats. But these feats are not super-human. Individuals capable of such acts have learned to use some of their innate potential, some of their natural power. It is a tragedy that individuals like Christ, Buddha, Mohammed and other great beings wind up being worshiped. How far more worthwhile it would be if they were emulated instead.

Powerful people come from all walks of life, and leave their mark on the world in a variety of ways. But one thing is common to them all. They move through the world with pure vitality. It is as though all their switches had been turned on. Following is a list of people who, in my estimation, either are or were powerful.

Albert Einstein—One of the greatest scientific geniuses in recorded history, Einstein developed the theory of relativity, contributed greatly to quantum theory, and dedicated much of his life to a unified-field theory. He won the Nobel Prize for physics in 1921. Einstein authored several books, and his work is credited as the groundbreaking material for huge areas of scientific endeavor, including the development of atomic power.

Alexander The Great—In recorded history there has never been as great a military leader. Alexander conquered the entire Persian empire. His empire spanned from the Indian Ocean to the Mediterranean Sea. There were several attempts to assassinate Alexander. Each attempt failed. Alexander systematically met and defeated armies of all sizes and nations. His entire campaign and all of his exploits occurred before he was thirty-three-years-old, when he died of a fever.

Therese Neumann—Born on Good Friday in 1898, this woman was blinded and paralyzed in an accident at age twenty. After fervent prayer to St. Therese of Lisieux, her sight and use of limbs were miraculously restored. From that point on, she accepted absolutely no food for the rest of her life, with the exception of one tiny, paper-thin consecrated wafer, taken daily at 6:00 A.M. Every Friday after her healing, Therese experienced the Passion of Christ, bleeding spontaneously and profusely from the hands, feet, head, and breast. During the weekly ordeal she lost 10 of her 120 pounds. Therese believed that her purpose was to demonstrate that humans can live on God's light alone. Her life story was documented by Dr. Fritz Gerlick.

Mohandas K. Gandhi—This unsuccessful Indian lawyer became the acknowledged leader of the entire Indian nation. An ascetic and celibate, Gandhi lived with a loincloth and shawl as his wardrobe. The ultimate pacifist, Gandhi led the *satyagraha* (holding to the truth)—a campaign of non-violent civil disobedience. He led agrarian-and labor-reform movements, and spun his own cloth as part of his campaign to revive industry in India. Gandhi led the first public campaign to mine domestic salt in India freely. Though jailed and abused repeatedly, Gandhi held to his convictions. When violence broke out in India, he fasted until the violence stopped. Such was his power that the public could not bear to have him die of hunger. His goal was a free Indian society, with abolition of the caste system. Gandhi was assassinated.

Rudolph Steiner—This Austrian born renaissance man was a prolific author, painter, sculptor, architect, and scientist. A renowned mystic, Steiner developed the science of Anthroposophy, a method of inquiry into higher worlds. He founded the Waldorf schools, a worldwide organization of educational institutions for children. He developed a system of anthroposophical medicine, which utilizes knowledge of the power of plant and mineral preparations. Steiner is the father of bio-dynamic farming, a method of organic agriculture which is used widely throughout Europe. Steiner was also a world authority on bees. His published works number in the hundreds.

Aboriginal Natives of Australia—These natives can fill an ostrich egg with water, bury it in the middle of the desert with no markings whatsoever, and find it quickly and easily two years later!

Tibetan Monks—Certain monks of the Mahayana Buddhist tradition practice *Tum-Mo*, a meditation on the inner fire. These monks sit in the freezing Himalayan snows, at high altitudes, in sub-zero temperatures, with no clothing on. In this condition they wrap themselves in sheets which have been soaked in water and frozen. The object of this practice is to generate enough inner fire to thaw out the sheets, and dry them completely. An accomplished practitioner can dry up to a dozen sheets in one night. This demonstration of their prowess proves that they have achieved a high level of Tum-Mo practice, the actual purpose of which is to arouse the inner fire in the body-mind, to break through blocks in the human energy circuits, and to achieve a state of self-realization.

Raja Sundernath—This man is known as a *Siddha*, a being of power. He lives in the Indian Himalayas, at high altitudes. He wears no clothing, has no home, and lives in the freezing snows. He has been living in this manner for decades, in excellent health.

Pygmies—These tiny African tribespeople can run over a hundred miles in pursuit of wild game.

Kikuyu Tribesmen—These Kenya natives can sit absolutely motionless in a tree for forty-eight hours.

"Running Buddhas"—The monks of Mt. Hiei in Japan undergo arduous training which includes a daily run of 52.5 miles over rugged terrain, each day for a hundred days. This is the equivalent of a double marathon each day for over three months! The same monks also undergo an "ultimate fast," during which they go without food, water, or sleep, for nine days. Medical science cannot explain why these monks live in a state of remarkable health. These monks are somewhat similar to the *lung-gom-pa* monks of Tibet, who could run two hundred miles without stopping or becoming tired.

What do all these people have in common? They live with unbending intent, they are strong-willed, and they are congruent. There is also a tremendous capacity to persist, to do what absolutely must be done, however strenuous or perilous.

What is at the seat of great genius, extraordinary physical prowess, and feats of endurance? As I mentioned before, there is a psycho-biological force, a body-mind power, within all of us. It is known by various names, such as *Chi*, *Ki*, *Shakti*, *Kundalini*, Orgone energy, Bioenergy, Godlight, *prana*, and more. Regardless of the name, power is within us. Furthermore, it can be cultivated, developed, and channeled. There are thousands of methods for accomplishing this.

What follows is about such methods. Yes, there are innumerable methods, but there are some which are choice. There are some which have a tang to them, that work readily and steadily. Some of those are assembled here. There is still more preliminary information to come; read it carefully. You need an understanding of what you are getting into to be successful with these methods. When you actually start to practice (if you do), believe in yourself and be persistent. Above all, be persistent.

2. The Cultivation of Power

"Until one is committed, there is hesitancy, the chance to draw back, always ineffectiveness. Concerning all acts of initiative (and creation), there is one elementary truth the ignorance of which kills countless ideas and splendid plans: that moment one definitely commits oneself, then Providence moves too. All sorts of things occur to help one that would never otherwise have occurred. A whole stream of events issues from the decision, raising in one's favor all manner of unforseen incidents and meetings and material assistance, which no man could have dreamed would come his way. Whatever you can do, or dream you can, begin it. Boldness has genius, power, and magic in it. Begin it now."— GOETHE

In ancient Oriental mythology, the dragon represents spirit and power. Both imperial and immortal, he is a master of the elements; he breathes fire, and is invincibly strong. A powerhouse of energy, the dragon is a winged serpent. As such, he is lord of the underworld, and ruler of the skies. The dragon is awesome, enormous, a law unto himself.

For thousands of years, the great sages of China, Tibet, and the Himalayas have learned to be like the dragon. By diligent practice and long years of exploration and study, the monks, wanderers, magicians, and warriors of the Orient have sought the supreme enlightenment of the human spirit. By their efforts, these individuals also become extraordinarily powerful. Feats of superhuman strength, perfect health, and long life are common among the sages, who have awakened and mastered the primal creative power and evolutionary force within all human beings. The power which sustains life, is also the source of intelligence and genius. Known as Chi, Ki, or Shakti, power can be aroused and increased within a person by performing various practices geared specifically toward that outcome.

Those who have awakened inner power are known as *Siddhas*, Beings of Power. Though many Siddhas live reclusively, some accept students and live in remote temples and villages, away from the distractions of the mundane world. Some live in urban areas, often incognito, known to a select few. There are in fact many Siddhas, individuals who have developed their inner power to an extraordinary degree.

Like the dragon, Siddhas are masters of the elements. Through herbology, martial arts, yoga, meditation, austerities, and study, the Siddha harnesses the forces of nature and becomes an elemental being. Just as the dragon is the lord of the underworld and ruler of the skies, the Siddha plumbs the innermost depths of human nature, and soars to the heights of the human spirit.

In the *Yoganusasanam*, the Great Yogic Sermon, it is said that "A warrior never bows to a gale—he rides upon its crest." This typifies the determination of those who seek to lead a life of power. But how does one proceed to accomplish this?

The dilemma which many people face is: Which path do I choose? Often the path chooses you. Circumstances occur and people come into one's life in such a way that a path is chosen as if it were pre-ordained. In fact, that may be the case. Still, other would-be students weigh one path against another, as if on a grandiose shopping expedition. How does one choose? It is not so much a matter of choosing one from another, but of learning many methods, assimilating what works, and dispensing with the rest. In other words, a path is not a thing to be chosen like a pair of shoes. It is a way which is cultivated. You could say that it is a custom fit. For the process of awakening is not the same for any two people. The nuances and peculiarities of one person's life may be of no concern to another. The way is fashioned according to individual needs.

The methods by which inner power can be awakened have historically been kept secret. Many methods have been developed and taught in remote, inaccessible areas, such as the sacred mountains of China, the Tibetan plateau, or the Himalayas. Until the development of modern transportation, these areas of the world were very hard to reach. Due to the nature of many practices, students often chose to train (in fact still do) in the most remote, undisturbed locations possible, away from human noise and interruption. Under such conditions, it is easier to attune oneself to the subtle cycles and rhythms of nature. It is also easier to develop the tremendous concentration needed for intensive psychic development. Also, because of the extremely powerful nature of many methods of awakening inner power, many teachings have been kept secret, taught only to those qualified to handle the intense energy generated by them.

Over time, secret teachings have "leaked out" to the general public. This has happened due to improved communication and travel in modern times. The publication of previously secret teachings has revolutionized the way people study. Ever greater numbers of people are learning to meditate, practice yoga, and study the martial arts, due to the increasing availability of material in recent times.

While a book cannot take the place of a living teacher, written materials can nonetheless be very valuable in the process of self-fulfillment. The methods in this book were at one time secret, and several have never been available to the general public in any form. They are all valuable tools for the development of the body-mind.

While many people consider the body and mind separately, they are actually one complete system. The body-mind is the workshop and the vehicle of the student. It is the terrain of the path, and represents the heavens and the earth. The body-mind is the laboratory of the alchemist, the battleground of the warrior, the magic kingdom of the sorcerer. Without the body-mind, there is nothing. For this reason, the student must learn to develop the body-mind to its full potential.

To engage in the deliberate and methodical development of power, one must be steadfast and determined to cultivate a lifestyle and attitude which actively support and further that pursuit. With this in mind, it is useful to make some personal resolutions which one can reflect upon daily. These resolutions are tools which elucidate some of the specific requirements for successful self-development. By reflecting upon them, one remains conscious of the process in which he or she is engaged. The following are resolutions which I find helpful in this regard:

• RESOLVE to pay diligent attention to the promotion of one's physical and spiritual health, to live in a manner which supports that well-being, and to avoid those actions or conditions which detract from it, except in such cases which demand the sacrifice of personal welfare for the achievement of a higher purpose.

• RESOLVE to feel and know oneself as integrally One with all of life, and to live in a manner which supports that union.

• RESOVE to keep the mind free of negativity toward others, and to take full responsibility for one's feelings, thoughts, and words.

• RESOLVE to live in the steadfast conviction that the true nature and worth of all human beings is in the Spirit.

• RESOLVE to carry out all resolutions with determination, courage, and a deep sense of duty, except in a case in which it can be shown that a resolution made is to the detriment of spiritual unfoldment.

• RESOLVE to see the good and the purpose in all that one is given, and to strive not to complain but to accept with gratitude the blessings and challenges in one's life.

• RESOLVE to strive continually and with great determination to regard life with deep reverence and respect, and to uphold the spiritual power of life to the best of one's ability.

Working with the body-mind system, there are methods of practice which seem to be strictly physical, or strictly mental. This is actually not the case. Performed correctly, all methods of physical culture serve to train the mind as well. Likewise, mental techniques help to develop the body. Thus in the practices which follow there is physical activity along with specific mental concentration.

The purpose of working with physical and mental faculties simultaneously is to develop the body-mind as one exquisitely sensitive mechanism, whose senses, strength, power, alertness, and ability to act are far more refined than those of an untrained person. With such a well-integrated body-mind, the student can then perceive, harness, and direct the most subtle spiritual forces. It is because of this refined development that many advanced students are great healers. The forces with which they work are also the energies of healing and regeneration.

In the following chapters, a model of the human being is given. There is a description of the human energy system, including the *chakras*, the major centers of energy in the body-mind. This description is only a model, which is to say that it is useful for understanding and performing the methods and techniques which follow. However, if you read a variety of books on yoga, the occult, or Taoism, you will find many descriptions of the human energy system, all of them somewhat different. The Chinese, for example, work a great deal with *meridians* of energy, invisible lines of force which run through the trunk and limbs of the body. The

Hindu Yogis, however, pay comparatively little attention to these meridians. Instead, they concentrate on the chakras, and a central line of energy which runs through the spine. The early Tibetans considered the knees to be major energy centers, an idea which is not shared by any other tradition. The Hopi Indians of North America use a model of the human energy system similar to that of the Hindu Yogis.

It is not important that there are many models of the human energy system. For there are methods of training which are suited to each model. What is important is that the model you are using works. If you are working with the chakra system, then your practice should enable you to experience the chakras, or the benefits attributed to them. Otherwise, either the model or your practice does not serve your needs.

In this book, the classical chakra model of the Kundalini Yogis is used. This is the system I have used for the last twenty years, and have taught to hundreds of students. It is powerful and effective. While the methods in this book come from a variety of traditions, they are all suitable to this chakra system. With careful practice, you will experience the chakras directly. Do not be concerned, then, with variations in energy models from one tradition to another. The models are vehicles for getting you to where you want to go.

There are three operating principles that are useful in developing power. The first is that the Universe is a friendly place to life. Einstein said this, and I believe it to be so. The Universe is a positive, generative place, intelligently created and operated. There is order, on earth and in the heavens, and that order is balanced, harmonious, and ecological. Just as the human body-mind is a generative, ecological system, so is the Universe. Understanding the Universe as a friendly place enables students of the spirit to appreciate their own place within the Cosmic order. To embrace this principle is not to deny that the world is mysterious, powerful, and dangerous. The world is vast and complex, with secrets enough for aeons of seekers to discover. The forces at play in the world are immensely powerful—wind, water, fire, the seasons, spirits, gods. These forces, plus unforeseen circumstances, make the world a dangerous place as well. Yet our world is one small particle in the fabric of the Universe.

The second operating principle is that life is a vast selection of opportunities. Human beings are designed to learn and grow. Our capacity to do so is determined by our attitude and awareness, and to a lesser extent by circumstances. At all times in one's life, the business of living is an opportunity to grow and develop. For many people, growth is random and haphazard, and a majority of growth opportunities go unused. Individuals trained to develop the body-mind, however, are keenly aware just how opportune each moment is. Such individuals have the resources to take full advantage of each moment. In addition, they develop the ability to pick and choose those circumstances which afford the greatest growth opportunities. By thinking of life as a vast selection of opportunities, one adds tremendous momentum to the process of learning. It is as though the world is a massive banquet, and we are seated at the feast.

The third operating principle is that you can do and be whatever you want. If you want to be well-educated, healthy, and rich, you can direct yourself in such a manner as to accomplish those goals. If you wish to grow the greenest lawn in your town, it can be done. If you wish to be an enlightened adept, you can. Whatever you want to do and be, you can. However, wishing does not make dreams come true. Rather, adequate planning and perseverance will bring your dreams to fruition. The potential of human beings is so great it is inconceivable. While many people are born to greatness, many more become great by diligence and labor. By accepting the principle of unlimited potential, the student overcomes many of the limiting beliefs which inhibit growth.

The three principles above are tools. They are useful for maximizing your efforts along the Path. They work, and they bring dramatic, positive results. As you initiate your own practice, take time to contemplate and embrace these principles. Doing so will help to make your practice rich and rewarding.

The methods in this book comprise an integrated approach to developing the body-mind. This is accomplished in several stages:

Strengthening the body—Specific exercises, such as the Chuang Fu methods of Buddha Hands Kung Fu, and the Five Tibetan techniques, strengthen and stretch the muscles, ligaments, and nerves of the body. By these practices, overall physical conditioning is achieved. Vitality is enhanced, and the nerves are prepared to carry greater energy.

Purifying and vitalizing the human energy system—The Ten Tibetan Breaths, The Five Elements Exercises, and the methods of Kundalini Yoga cleanse the body of impurities and remove blockages from its energy channels. These methods activate the chakras, generating tremendous physical and psychic vitality. This precedes the arousal of the *Kundalini Shakti*, the primordial creative energy which lies at the base of the spine, and which is the evolutionary force within all human beings.

Training and clearing the mind—The methods of Solar Plexus Charging, Energy Polarization, and Meditation develop the ability to concentrate and focus the mind. This training leads to the ability to clear the mind, to become thought-free, so that rarified psychic energy can flow unobstructed as pure consciousness.

Employing magic—The Invocation Of The Shadow is a magic technique which enables the student to utilize subtle psychic forces simply and quickly, with none of the hocus-pocus associated with ritual magic. As practice with the shadow develops, one's intuitive faculties become more attuned. Magic is then understood for what it really is—a particular formula for getting things done.

Cultivating body-mind synthesis—All of the methods described in this book work with the body-mind as a whole system. Through practice, the illusion of the separation between body and mind disappears. The bridge between them is built and strengthened, and they function as one. When this is accomplished, power is readily aroused and channeled.

Dietary considerations—While diet is extremely important in the care and maintenance of the body-mind, it is not covered in this book. In my previous book, *Take Charge of Your Health: Healing with Yogatherapy and Nutrition*, I cover diet in great detail. Since that volume gives extensive recommendations for eating, the use of supplements, and the use of herbs, I do not duplicate that material here.

There is an occult saying that energy follows thought. As we think, so is our energy directed. Thought affects our feelings and behavior. One of the challenges of any spiritual undertaking is to shape our thinking so that we direct our mental energy toward that which we wish to accomplish. To shape our thinking in this way, *Intent*, *Will*, and *Congruency* are very important.

Intent is fixed attention. If you are engaged in work as demanding as the full development of power, you must work with what Don Juan, in Carlos Castaneda's remarkable series of books, calls "unbending intent." To develop power is to totally revolutionize the way that you live. Your life will be changed forever. To realize such change requires constant attention to the process by which those changes occur. Every day, moment to moment, your intent must be to fulfill that revolution. If you are practicing your martial art, you intend to be as precise and powerful as you can. If you are chopping vegetables, you intend to be as conscious as possible. Your intent is the thread which holds your practice together, and which leads to fulfillment of your goals. When your intent is focused, you remember your purpose at all times. To develop unbending intent, you first must decide what it is that you want. Do you want to assume the task of developing the body-mind to a very fine degree? You will probably need to know something about what is required to do that, before determining if that is what you want. The more you learn the more you will understand what kind of work is involved. Your intent will change and develop as you become more informed.

Will is the power that you add to intent to accomplish your goals. Will is sheer determination. It is drive and certainty. Will is the ability to neutralize distraction. In the world there are millions of distractions which can influence a person away from the process of generating power. When you will to fulfill your purpose, that power acts as a concentrated fuel for action. Will is the cutting edge of the finely honed mind. When you are committed to a particular course of action, will is the power to stay on course, no matter what contrary or adverse conditions may arise.

One way to develop will is to develop a track record of fulfilling whatever you intend. For example, if you are considering seriously pursuing spiritual practices, then work into that pursuit in stages. Decide, for example, that you will devote half-an-hour each day for a month to study and reading on the subject. Make sure that you follow through with this. Then, try something more demanding. For example, commit to meditating for forty-five minutes every day, for six months. Do this without fail. Set time lines, and keep them. Gradually you will develop your will, so that when you commit to even bigger, more strenuous pursuits, you will be determined enough to follow through. Whatever you decide to do, do it for yourself. Do not undertake any of this process because someone else tells you that you should. Do it because it makes sense, because you want to.

Congruency is consistency. To be congruent is to live such that you think, feel, and act in a manner absolutely consistent with your intent. To be congruent is to live harmoniously, so that all that you are and all that you do fits together smoothly, without counterproductive elements. If, for example, you wish to be in perfect health, then you would not drink alcohol to excess. It is not that drinking is morally wrong, but drinking to excess is not congruent with the desire to be perfectly healthy. On the other hand, you would choose to exercise regularly, because that activity is congruent with the desire for perfect health. You can think of being congruent as similar to traveling on a highway. When the pavement is smooth, traffic is light, the weather is dry, and your car is in excellent running order, then your driving will likely be smooth and steady. However, if there are potholes in the road, it is raining, and your car is in disrepair, then your driving will be problematic. Being congruent allows for the smooth, steady operation of one's own life, whereas being incongruent creates conflict within oneself.

This is not to state or imply that the individual who is congruent encounters no difficulties in life. There will still be unforeseen events, strange occurrences, and possibly accident and misfortune. But at least many personally generated problems can be prevented. And, there is something else. When you are congruent, you develop tremendous personal power. This is because you do not "leak" your power through counterproductive activities. So your power grows and grows. It is steady and consistent.

I would like to add a few words about attitude. If something is not enjoyable, why do it? I have met a great many people engaged in one form of spiritual practice or another, who are very dour and grim about the whole business. As far as I am concerned, that is crazy. Being overly serious is one of the surest ways to poison one's life. What are we here for, if not to enjoy ourselves? Yes, it is true that the world is a dangerous place. Yes, it is also true that to awaken to real power is a monumental undertaking. Do this work earnestly, with full effort, but do not take yourself too seriously.

We never stop growing. There is really no absolute goal, no end of the road, no final enlightenment. "Mastery" is a never-ending, ever-changing reference to the best that we can possibly be. In this work you do not finish the job, slap the dust off your hands, and walk away. There are always other aspects of ourselves to develop.

Finally, remember that power is just a name, a way of thinking about the world, a way of orienting oneself to the condition of being alive in this Universe. Do not get hung up on it.

3. The Human Energy System

The human body-mind system is the most complex, intelligently designed system on earth. Human beings exhibit all the abilities of other animals, including food gathering, reproduction, survival skills, and adaptation. However, we far exceed all other known species as far as intelligence and communication are concerned. A lion cannot return from a long hunting trip and sit down with members of its pride and describe the events of the day. A human can do that with ease. A dog cannot invent or manufacture a computer. We humans thrive on invention. For all of our shortcomings, including our propensity toward violence, greed, and cruelty, we are a fundamentally intelligent species, and the most sophisticated animal on this planet of ours. We have made more changes on the planet than all other species combined, and we also have the capacity to destroy the whole place.

The human body-mind is sophisticated. On a physical level, the human body is exquisitely well-engineered, with digestive, reproductive, cardiovascular, skeletal, and nervous systems without par. We are so well-engineered that we can perform a wider range of physical functions than any other creature. Our dexterity is such that we can adapt to virtually any environment or condition, if we have enough time to prepare for it. While it is true that we can not fly or remain underwater without special apparatus, our physical capabilities are so extensive that we can actually build whatever apparatus we need. Beavers build dams, birds build nests, and termites build hills. But humans build superhighways, jet planes, submarines, rockets, skyscrapers, and dams.

The magnificent human body is powered by the even more amazing human brain. Absolutely the most intelligent apparatus known, the human brain takes in, processes, and generates trillions of bits of information every day! The brain powers the body, making sure that all systems work. Breathing must continue constantly, and it must be coordinated with cardiovascular activity. Messages for this are sent via the nervous system. The digestive system processes and metabolizes foodstuffs—all at the brain's command. Even though the brain must operate the functions of the body without a break, twenty-four hours daily, it still has loads of capacity to think. And think it does. Our brains can process information better than any computer ever built. Plus, our brains can generate original material. From songs to stories to words to inventions, our brains come up with new things all the time.

The body and brain, as remarkable as they are, represent only part of the body-mind. The body-mind is the whole human, and that includes the mind, and the rest of the human energy system. The mind is consciousness itself. Its vehicle within the body is the brain, but the mind has a life of its own, one which goes further than its bodily residence. The mind is one of many vehicles which make up who it is that we are. While the subject of the mind is interesting and important, we will not dwell on it here. That topic can occupy more volumes than any one person could write.

Our focus instead is on the human energy system. The human energy system is the substrate of the body-mind. It is a system within a system, non-physical, but no less real than our arms, legs, stomachs. The human energy system is very much like the physical nervous system. It is similar in design, and in operation. Like the physical nervous system, the human energy system runs throughout the entire bodily vehicle. It has major and minor pathways, just like nerves. The nervous system has major bunches of nerves called *plexuses*. The human energy system has chakras, centers where the energy pathways converge and concentrate power. Just as the nervous system conducts trillions of impulses to keep the body running correctly, the human energy system conducts trillions of impulses of energy to keep the nervous system and the body going. There is nothing theoretical about the human energy system. Without it no human being could live. It is even more basic than our blood and bones.

Unlike the nervous system, the human energy system extends beyond the borders of the physical body. In addition, the human energy system can be activated, influenced, and used by the mind very easily. This in turn affects the activity of the body.

Think of it this way. Your body and brain are filled with a very fine webbing which completely penetrates the entire physical vehicle. This webbing is made of energy. The energy is well organized, and intelligently operated. This energy system, as we call it, actually operates the physical person. It empowers the physical body, and it is the interface between the body and pure intelligence. It is the medium through which pure life-energy flows.

The Chakra System

As mentioned in Chapter 2, the chakra system I use is that of classical Hindu Kundalini Yoga. There are other systems. However, this is the one with which I am most familiar. It is the most widely known of all the chakra systems, and it has very specific correlations to components of the physical body. Most importantly, this chakra system works. Why should you care about the chakras at all? By working with them, by becoming familiar with how they operate, and by experiencing accelerated activity in the chakra system, your whole world will change dynamically. Your ability to direct your energy to whatever you want, is the value of getting to know the chakras.

The chakras are vortices of energy. Throughout the entire body-mind system, there are many points of concentrated energy, but the seven chakras are the major vortices in the whole system. Lying along the spinal pathway, the chakras are the main centers of energy distribution for the rest of the human energy system. Each chakra is associated with specific organs, glands, and nerves. In addition, each chakra relates to a specific aspect of human consciousness. For example, the third chakra is related to will and personal power, while the sixth chakra is related to insight and higher intelligence. All physical functions, as well as all aspects of human consciousness, are associated with the chakras.

The seven chakras work together, as do the organs and glands of the body. Just like organs and glands, the chakras can be weak or strong, in perfect balance, or imbalanced. They can function well or poorly. However, the chakras can be easily influenced. That is why there are methods of power to balance, strengthen, and optimize chakra activity. The ideal situation is for each of these vortices to be at peak activity and condition, in perfect balance with each other. Leading a "balanced life" contributes to this balance in the chakra system. It is a building process. Behavior affects the chakras, which further affect behavior, which further affects the chakras. For each person, balance is a unique affair. Discovering one's own balance is what the path of self-development is really all about. For balance is a delicate condition, and it is affected by influences which change constantly.

Ida, Pingala, Sushumna

The seven chakras lie along the spinal path. They are connected by the three major energy pathways in the complete human energy system, the *Ida*, *Pingala*, and *Sushumna*. These three channels run from the very base of the spine to the top of the head. Sushumna is the central channel. Sushumna is to the entire human energy system what the spinal cord is to the physical body. It is the very core of all operations. It is the main connection between the chakras. It is the pathway by which energy travels from the base of the spine to the top of the head. It is through Sushumna that the Kundalini energy (described further on) travels, illuminating the body-mind.

At the base of the spine, at the location of the first chakra, is the origin of Sushumna and the other two channels, Ida and Pingala. Ida starts on the left side of Sushumna, while Pingala starts on the right. Ida and Pingala travel upward, intertwining with each other at each chakra. Ida is connected with the left nostril, while Pingala is connected with the right. Ida is related to the lunar force (Yin), while Pingala is related to the solar force (Yang). The symbol of the medical profession, the caduceus, is actually a representation of these three major energy pathways. It is usually represented as a staff with two serpents winding around it, leading up to a pair of wings—symbolic of the two petals of the *Third Eye*, or Wisdom Eye. These three energy channels have been known for thousands of years.

The First Chakra, Muladhara

The first chakra is named *Muladhara*. It is located at the base of the spine, at the *perineum*, between the anus and the genitals. Its associated organs are the large intestine and the rectum. Its associated glands are the adrenal glands. Its major related nerve center is the sacral plexus. The primary functions of the first chakra are survival, power, the promotion of vital life-energy, and elimination.

This chakra is associated with the most basic aspects of human survival. The energy flowing through it is dense, vital, and powerful. Survival is a tendency which is imprinted into our genetic makeup. It is at the root of our consciousness. We each have a reptilian inner brain, the main function of which is to promote survival. To do anything else, we must survive. The first chakra is at the root of the spine, and the influence of the first chakra is at the root of all human consciousness.

The Second Chakra, Svadhisthana

The second chakra is called *Svadhisthana*. It is located at the spine, close to the genitals. Its associated organs are the large intestine, the bladder, kidneys, and the genitals. It is associated with all the reproductive glands. Its major related nerve centers are the prostatic plexus (male), or the utero-vaginal plexus (female). The primary functions of the second chakra are survival, procreation, sexual function, and the promotion of vitality.

Creativity occurs in many ways, in many activities. The most fundamental human creativity is the act of procreation. The second chakra is the center of sexual energy, of procreation and regeneration. Sexual energy is a creative force. Its influence goes beyond sexual activity to thought, feelings, behavior, art, music, fashion, even architecture and automotive design. Sexual orgasm is both a basic experience of biological satisfaction and a transcendental experience. One of the reasons that sexual orgasm is so highly regarded is that during orgasm one experiences, however briefly, a sense of timelessness. It is this same timeless sense which is common to mystical states. The second chakra is a highly active center, the energy from which permeates almost everything that we are or do. It is involved with both basic creativity and higher ecstasy.

The Third Chakra, Manipura

The third chakra is named *Manipura*. It is located at the spine, across from the solar plexus. Its associated organs are the liver, spleen, stomach, and small intestines. Its associated gland is the pancreas. Its major related nerve center is the solar plexus. The primary functions of the third chakra are will, personal power, digestion, and assimilation of nutrients.

The third chakra is the strongest center of the individual self, and of the will. Individuation of consciousness goes beyond basic survival and continuation of the species, to a sense of oneself as a unique being. The third chakra is the vortex of power for the individuation of consciousness. It is the center of personal power. Will originates from this chakra. It is this chakra which generates self-assertion, personal determination, and individual strength. It is the third chakra which prepares us to meet the challenges of living in the world. This center can be enormously powerful, and is associated with the phenomenon known as *charisma*.

The Fourth Chakra, Anahata

The fourth chakra is named *Anahata*. It is located at the spine, across from the *sternum* (center of the chest). Its associated organs are the heart and lungs. Its associated gland is the thymus gland. Its major related nerve center is the cardiac plexus. The primary functions of the fourth chakra are love, compassion, immunity, heart, lung, and bronchial functions.

The fourth chakra is known as the center of love and compassion. It is at this center that human consciousness makes a leap beyond self-centeredness. The energy which flows from this center is directed beyond personal survival, to consideration of others. The fourth chakra is a vortex of expanded awareness, of connection with the rest of the world. It is also the mid-point between the lower triangle (chakras 1, 2, 3) and the higher three centers, and is the conscious point of departure from lower to higher awareness. To gain access to the higher functions of creativity and awareness, one must "pass through" the fourth chakra.

The Fifth Chakra, Visuddha

The fifth chakra is named *visuddha*. It is located at the spine, in the center of the throat. Its associated organs are the vocal cords. Its associated gland is the thyroid. Its major related nerve center is the pharyngeal plexus. The primary functions of the fifth chakra are higher creativity and speech.

The energy for the higher functions of creativity, artistic expression, and speech, flow through the fifth chakra. The force of this vortex is most noticeable in the activity of speaking. When this chakra is well developed, one can speak with tremendous force and influence. Speech may well be the single most influential human behavior. All creative activity, from painting to writing to playing music, involves a process by which we express something from within. When creative energies of the fifth chakra are strong, such expression can be dramatic, powerful, deeply moving. This chakra is so potent that the force flowing from it can be spellbinding.

The Sixth Chakra, Ajna

The sixth chakra is named *Ajna*. It is located at the center of the head, directly behind the root of the nose, between the brows. Its associated organ is the brain. Its associated gland is the pituitary. Its primary related nerve center is the cavernous plexus. The primary functions of the sixth chakra are higher intelligence, clairvoyance, insight, and refined hearing.

Also known as the Third Eye or Wisdom Eye, this chakra is the location of higher intelligence and supranormal vision. The Third Eye is truly the center of insight, an inner vision directed by wisdom and a deep understanding of the subtle forces at play in any situation. When the Third Eye is "open," one can see the past, present, and future clearly. Individuals with this extraordinary vision are the few true clairvoyants and sages who have lived among humanity throughout history. The higher intelligence associated with the sixth chakra is exquisitely balanced and sensitive. An open Third Eye enables one to achieve desired outcomes easily, and to desire outcomes which are positive and generative.

The Seventh Chakra, Sahasrara

The seventh chakra is named *Sahasrara*. It is located at the crown of the head. Its associated organ is the brain. Its associated gland is the pineal. Its major related nerve center is the cavernous plexus. The primary function of the seventh chakra is cosmic consciousness.

Cosmic consciousness is a condition of total fulfillment. It is absolute awareness and integration with the primary, creative force of the Universe. It is an unconditional state of freedom, wisdom, energy, insight, and joy. Cosmic consciousness is also the natural human condition upon the awakening of the seventh chakra. Such awakening is usually the product of intensive purification, inner refinement, and spiritual work. However, since cosmic consciousness, or illumination, or enlightenment, cannot be known by the intellect, one cannot say that there are only so many ways to attain this condition. The truth is, genuine illumination is outside the scope of intellectual thought. It can only be known by experiencing it. So maybe there are myriad ways to be enlightened. I cannot say.

Kundalini

Now you have some basic understanding of the chakra system, including the three major energy pathways—Ida, Pingala, and Sushumna—and the seven major energy vortices. There is a great deal more to the human energy system, but before we move on to the meridians and the aura, it is helpful at this time to consider the power which moves through the system.

The human energy system exists because there is a need for a structure, a complex circuitry, through which the fundamental power of life can flow. This power has many names. It is called bio-energy, Chi, Ki, The Force, and a thousand other terms. Names vary from one culture to another, from one mystical school to another, from language to language. For the purposes of being consistent with the Hindu description of the human energy system, I will use the term Kundalini.

The word "Kundalini" invokes curiosity, fear, suspicion, and confusion. Kundalini is misunderstood, primarily due to wild stories and folk tales which have been told about this force. For starters, Kundalini is the primary life-force, the primary evolutionary force, and the seat of genius in all human beings. Kundalini is the most potent force within us. The Kundalini is often referred to as The Serpent Power, because it is said to be coiled like a snake. Whether or not this is actually the case, the Kundalini resides at the base of the spine, at the first chakra, Muladhara.

Because Kundalini was first discovered thousands of years ago, much of what is written about this force is clothed in archaic language and outmoded ideas. Kundalini is often referred to as a goddess, for starters. I do not believe that there is any need for deification of this force. Nor is there a need to assign to it some specific personality. People of ancient cultures gave names and identities to a wide array of natural forces and phenomena. The wind, sun, rain—all had names, all were ruled by gods and goddesses. I think we can move beyond that. As far as I am concerned, Kundalini is the primary psycho-biological force. In other words, Kundalini is THE energy of the body-mind.

Kundalini is active all the time. There is some literature which states that the Kundalini Shakti (power) is dormant, inactive, until a person practices certain body-mind disciplines. This is not the case. The Kundalini is active twenty-four hours a day. It fuels the entire human energy system, and circulates energy through us all on a continuous basis. However, the activity of Kundalini in most people is minimal compared to what it could be. You can compare the Kundalini to electricity. For most people, the Kundalini Shakti runs at about 110 volts. But it has the capacity to operate at a power in excess of 50,000 volts. In fact, the potential force of the Kundalini Shakti is massive, beyond comprehension.

What the practice of body-mind disciplines does is to strengthen the "nerves" of the human energy system, break down energy blockages in the system, and make way for an increased flow of Kundalini Shakti. As this process occurs, the Kundalini energy may reach its 50,000-volt potential. Specific methods and systems, such as the ones in this book, open up the chakras. When the chakras are highly activated, they can handle an increased Kundalini flow.

The rising of Kundalini energy can happen in several ways. It can be slow, smooth, and imperceptible, such that over a long period of time you very gently increase total body-mind energy. Another possibility is that you will feel surges of Kundalini, as though some warm fluid were gently flowing up your spine. Such sensations are relatively common among practitioners of methods of power. The Kundalini Shakti can also rise like lightning, with intense heat and energy blasting up the spinal centers. Its arousal may be quick and sudden, and the intensity of the energy flow may incapacitate a person. If the Kundalini force rises quickly and powerfully, a person may spontaneously move in and out of a broad repertoire of yoga postures—even with little or no prior training.

It is because of the powerful phenomena associated with Kundalini arousal that this force has developed a strange reputation over the past few centuries. However, if you practice methods of power regularly and sensibly, you will be fairly well prepared to accept increased Kundalini flow. I say "fairly well prepared" because you cannot really be fully prepared for something as immense as Kundalini. It can surprise the strongest and best-developed people. If you really unlock a potent flow of Kundalini, then the best thing to do is go with the experience; do not resist it. Kundalini is stronger than anything else you know about.

For most people, Kundalini arousal will be smooth and steady, with few or no "lightning" type experiences. Meditation is the best practice for arousing Kundalini and preparing oneself for it.

Meridians

As you have learned, there are three major spinal energy pathways. There are also twelve major meridians—energy pathways which travel to and through major organs. These meridians run vertically through the body, and supply energy and vitality to organs, muscles, and "zones" of the body-mind system. The meridians are key to the practice of acupuncture. In that science, there are specific points which lie along the meridians. These acupuncture points are where a needle is inserted or fingertip pressure is applied to restore balance and vitality to a person. The science of acupuncture is tied in with the entire system of traditional Chinese medicine. This includes the theory of the Five Elements, or *Wu-Hsing*. See chapter 6 for information about the Five Elements.

The meridians are named after anatomical parts. Their names are the Lung, Large Intestine, Stomach, Spleen, Heart, Small Intestine, Bladder, Kidney, Pericardium, Triple Warmer, Gall Bladder, and Liver meridians. The meridians intensify and decrease in energy over a twenty-four-hour period. Energy travels through one meridian to another in an endless cycle, continuously. If there is an imbalance of any kind in the body-mind, there is some obstruction or imbalance among the meridians. Diet, special exercises, acupuncture, herbs, and meditation can be used to restore balance and improve energy flow.

The cycle by which the meridians intensify is as follows:

- Lung Meridian   3–5 A.M.
- Large Intestine Meridian   5–7 A.M.

- Stomach Meridian   7–9 A.M.
- Spleen Meridian   9–11 A.M.
- Heart Meridian   11 A.M.–1 P.M.
- Small Intestine Meridian   1–3 P.M.
- Bladder Meridian   3–5 P.M.
- Kidney Meridian   5–7 P.M.
- Pericardium Meridian   7–9 P.M.
- Triple Warmer Meridian   9–11 P.M.
- Gall Bladder Meridian   11 P.M.–1 A.M.
- Liver meridian   1–3 A.M.

In addition to the twelve major meridians described above, there are also the Conception Vessel and Governing Vessel meridians. The Governing Vessel runs all the way from the perineum (between the anus and genitals), up the spine, over the top of the head, to the upper lip. It follows almost exactly the Kundalini line through the chakras. The Conception Vessel meridian runs from the lower lip down to the perineum. The loop made by these two meridians is known to the Taoists, the sages of China, as the Microcosmic Orbit. In the Taoist meditation system, this energy loop is opened up, and the energy which circulates runs up the back, through the Governing vessel, and down the front, through the Conception Vessel. The opening of the Microcosmic Orbit is critical to success in Taoist meditation.

For our purposes, it is unnecessary to dwell on the meridians. They are useful concepts though, and I recommend that readers pick up a couple of books on Oriental medicine and acupuncture, to learn more about these energy pathways, and how they are related to health. The many methods in this book do in fact balance the energy of the meridians, especially the Five Elements Exercises, and the Five Tibetans. However, to understand the meridians better, do take time to read more about them.

The Aura

The aura is the last part of the human energy system to be described here. The *aura* is a psycho-electromagnetic field which surrounds the entire body-mind. It extends beyond the borders of the physical body, and it is luminous. The aura is the subject of many decades of investigation, and has been measured and photographed. It is visible to a small percentage of people, though one can train to see the aura.

The aura is a human rainbow-body. It is colorful, and each color has a different significance, indicating something about the health, vitality, or mental condition of a person. The size, shape, brilliance, and colors of the aura are all determined by who we are, how we feel, what we think. A vital, positive, dynamic person will have a brilliant, gleaming, large aura. In contrast, an unhappy, tired, sickly person will have a dull, thin, murky aura. When we feel a person's presence, it is their aura that we sense.

The aura is also a shield. It is a semi-permeable membrane, through which only certain vibrations may pass. Exactly which vibrations or energies may pass through

36

the aura depends entirely upon the condition of that luminous sheath. A strong, brilliant aura will let in only positive, health-bestowing energies, and will deflect unhealthy energies. By practicing methods of power, you build up an ever-stronger aura, and thus you become accessible only to generative forces.

The aura is as much a part of us as our arms and legs. It is an extension of the human energy system, and is the first part of us to interact with the environment. The aura is like a fingerprint made of energy instead of loops and swirls. Unlike a fingerprint, though, your aura can change completely. While there are certain identifying characteristics of each individual soul reflected in the aura which do not change, still the size, shape, color, and brilliance of the aura are altered with regular practice of empowering techniques.

4. Power of the Breath

Breath is life. Breathing is a simple, automatic function. We breath from the moment we are born. When we stop breathing, we die. We humans are very versatile and adaptable. We can go without food for prolonged periods, as evidenced by some of the great fasting heroics of Gandhi. We can go without water for a few days. We can go without pizza, movies, even sex, for extended periods. The monks of Mt. Hiei in Japan, as mentioned before, actually go without sleep for a period of nine days. If, however, you try to go without breathing for an extended period of time, you will be released from your mortal form.

When we breathe, we take in oxygen, which is needed to feed our cells. We also take in *prana*, the subtle energy of the breath. Just as oxygen feeds the cells of our bodies, prana feeds the human energy system, the energy sub-structure of the human body-mind. Breathing is the most primary form of human nourishment. We breathe to live.

Though breathing is a simple and natural function, it can be manipulated to obtain particular results. Not only does prana from the breath feed the energy circuits and chakras within us, but it can be channeled and used to build, purify, and strengthen the entire human energy system. Thus virtually every system of body-mind development, from yoga to the martial arts, employs methods of breath control. It is said that when you master the breath, you master your destiny. Whether this is actually so, it is certain that when you master the breath, you can exercise tremendous control over your entire body-mind.

In this chapter, a series of breathing techniques is presented. Some of the methods are simple. Some are more complex, and more powerful. But you should know that even the simplest methods of breath control should be practiced carefully, according to the directions given here. There is often a temptation to do more, to start practicing with great intensity, doing ten times more than what is recommended. Do a thousand push-ups if you need to feel that you are accelerating your progress. But **DO NOT** overdo breathing. Breathing methods are deceivingly powerful. Because breathing is something that we do naturally, it may seem as though playing around with the breath is of little consequence. I assure you, this is not the case. If you want to progress well in developing the body-mind, and if you wish to develop your practice properly, please carefully follow the directions given for the breathing techniques that follow.

Breathing is a complete yoga system unto itself, and there are endless variations to *pranayam*, the science of breath control. The following methods of pranayam are, in my opinion, the *creme de la creme* of all the methods I have encountered. I have practiced all of these methods for extended periods of time, and find that they increase energy, enhance mental clarity, purify the body-mind, improve sleep, and hone the senses.

As with any other practice, pranayam takes time to develop well. When you engage in breathing exercises, a number of things begin to occur. Your body begins to detoxify, and poisons are expelled from the liver, kidneys, bowels, and skin. You may feel light-headed during pranayam, and that is due to the greatly increased amount of oxygen going to your brain. But the sensation of lightness is not strictly chemical. As you breathe, you break through subtle (and sometimes not so subtle) blocks in the human energy system. Blocks along nerves, or near the chakras, are dissolved with consistent pranayam. As the human energy system begins to conduct more energy, you will feel lighter. Sometimes it seems as though each and every cell of your being is dancing in light.

This is actually the case. Each atomic particle of your being is suspended in space, and is dancing around other atomic particles at a rapid rate. Becoming "lighter" is not only a matter of being less heavy, but also of assimilating more light through the breath. With controlled breathing, you draw in pure, clear, white light into the body-mind, through the chakra system. At first this idea may seem quaint, or like the mumbo jumbo which typifies many spiritual systems. But consider that all of creation is actually energy and light. Matter is not really solid, but is a form of heavy, condensed energy. When you draw in the breath, doesn't it stand to reason that you are actually drawing in more energy and light?

Practice pranayam on a relatively empty stomach. This is for two reasons. When the stomach is full and you perform breathing exercises, nausea and cramping often occur. Secondly, when your system is not engaged in digestion, there is more energy available to assimilate the nourishment of the breath.

So . . . let's begin!

The Normal Breath: Sit in a comfortable position, either cross-legged or in a
straight chair. Keep your spine erect, so you are sitting tall and straight. The
shoulders and chest are relaxed. Place one hand on your abdomen. Take a light
breath through the nose, and as you do, let the abdomen fill and extend outward.
The chest should not move at all. This breath is like filling a balloon. As you
inhale, the abdomen expands. As you exhale, it collapses. This is very important.
Go over this again and again. For about two minutes, practice easy, gentle breathing, expanding the abdomen as you inhale, and collapsing it as you exhale. This is
the relaxed breathing that you should maintain during the day. You do not need
to continually practice this breath with your hand on your abdomen. Initially,
however, that helps to monitor the breath.

   Note: It is important to inhale through the nose, as inhaling through the
mouth bypasses energy regulating mechanisms in the body-mind, and can lead to
imbalances including physical and emotional problems. Be sure to inhale regularly
through the nose. Exhalation may be either through the nose or mouth.

The Long Deep Breath: This is similar to the normal breath, except that it is
deeper. This time, put one hand on your abdomen, and one in the middle of your
chest. This is only for learning the breath correctly, not for regular practice. As
you take a breath, fill your abdomen as before in the Normal Breath. Continue
the breath until your lungs are also full, and your chest is expanded. Then gently
exhale. It is important that you work with this breath until you perform it correctly, easily. The Long Deep Breath is much like filling a glass of water. You
pour water in from the top, but the glass fills from the bottom up. It is the same
with the breath. Breath comes in from the top
of your body, but you fill up from
your lower abdomen, and then your chest.
Practice this for several minutes every
day, until you have perfected the breath.

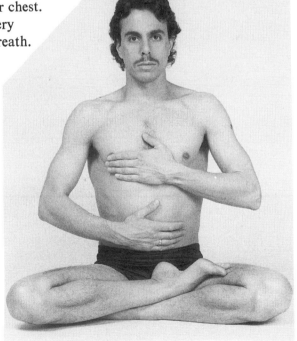

Tension Release Breath: I learned this breath from Swami Rudrananda, or Rudi, as most people called him. This breath is useful for releasing tension and stress-related garbage from your system.

Sit cross-legged with your spine straight. Your arms are out to the sides, bent at the elbows, with your hands hanging loosely at the wrists. Take a long, deep, full breath and hold it. Holding the breath, shake your arms and hands vigorously (Rudi said to shake as though you are shaking off shit), for about fifteen seconds or so. Repeat this three times, and then relax for a minute.

The Tension Release Breath is useful after work, or any time you wish to shed tension.

The Breaths of Buddha Hands

Buddha Hands Kung Fu is a powerful system of combat which is said to have originated in Tibet about 4,000 years ago. In the following chapter on Chuang Fu, a brief explanation and history of Buddha Hands is given. For the purposes of this chapter, it is worthy of note that Buddha Hands is not only a system of combat, but is also a complete system of training the body-mind. Included in the system are meditations, Tibetan yoga exercises, and breathing techniques. There are four breaths in particular which are used in Buddha Hands training.

Since it is not possible to practice a martial art from a book, I make no attempt here to present the entire system of Buddha Hands. However, the breathing methods can be used as a yoga practice by themselves. You can incorporate them into any yoga, martial arts, or exercise routine, or simply practice them by themselves.

Training Breathing

Sit cross-legged, with your spine straight and shoulders relaxed. This breath is
between the Normal Breath, and the Long Deep Breath. You breathe as you would
in the Long Deep Breath, but do not fill yourself completely. You inhale through
the nose. Exhalation is through the mouth, with your lips like a pipe. The exhalation is twice as long as the inhalation. As you breathe, let yourself be both
relaxed and alert at the same time. You can engage in Training Breathing for
several minutes.

Training Breathing is particularly useful when you are "cooling down" after
vigorous exercise. It is also helpful if you simply want to calm yourself. Training
Breathing has a soothing, balancing effect upon the body-mind.

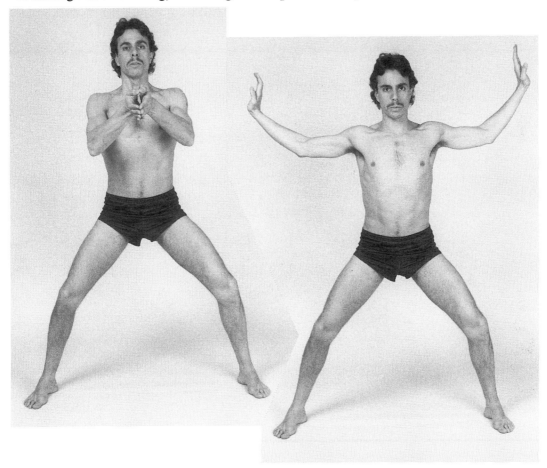

Open Lotus Breathing

Stand in the Horse Stance (See page 56), with your feet wider apart than shoulder's
width. Your feet are parallel to each other, your knees are bent and wide apart.
Your back is straight, with a small inward curve in the lower spine. With your
hands in a lotus (see photo) at the level of your abdomen, begin to inhale deeply.

As you inhale, push your hands up toward the sky, until your arms are almost straight. As you exhale through the mouth, your lips are like a pipe, so the breath pushes out forcefully. As you exhale, trace an arc with your arms out to the sides, until your hands are resting on your hips. This breath is full and powerful. Practice it energetically, three times.

Open Lotus Breathing opens up the lungs, and enhances your awareness of the space around you.

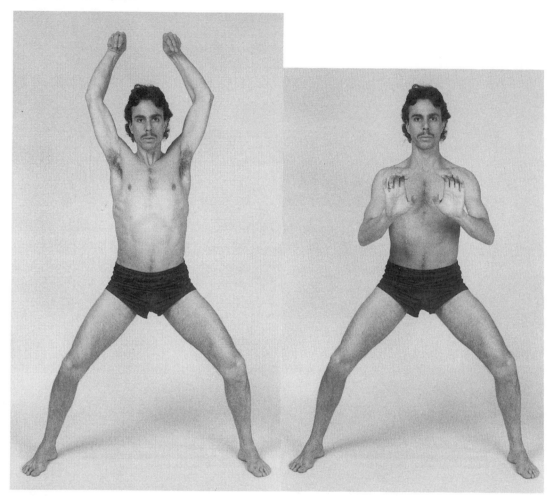

Snake Breathing

Standing in the Horse Stance (See page 56), your hands are together in front of your groin, with the fingers together and the backs of your hands facing outward. As you inhale deeply through the nose, extend your arms upward, with the hands bent down at the wrists. Exhale through the mouth, making a hissing sound. Exhale completely, pulling your hands down toward your groin, with the palms facing outward. Perform this breath vigorously three times. Snake Breathing is a concentrated breath which opens the lungs, and heightens alertness.

Flying Crane Breathing

Stand in the Horse Stance (See page 56), with your hands in a lotus in front of your abdomen. As you inhale deeply, push your arms up toward the sky, until they are almost straight. As you exhale, with your lips like a pipe, extend the arms to the sides, hands bent at the wrists. While still exhaling, float your arms down, rotating your hands in a forward direction, as though your hands were wings. Practice this breath three times. Flying Crane Breathing is a cooling, soothing breath which opens the lungs, and relaxes as well.

n the early 1900s a geographer named Dingle became critically ill while completing a detailed topographical survey of China. Dingle developed a high fever, and lapsed into unconsciousness. Upon awakening from this state, he was surprised to discover that he had been taken to Tibet, and was in the care of a high Tibetan Lama who, Dingle realized, had been his spiritual master in a previous lifetime.

In addition to nursing Dingle back to health, the Lama taught him a system of powerful Tibetan breathing exercises. This powerful system of yoga transformed Dingle's life, and revolutionized his sense of purpose. After a brief nine months under the Lama's tutelage, Dingle returned to the United States, where he founded the Science Of Mentalphysics.

At its height, Mentalphysics was a huge organization boasting one hundred thousand students throughout the world. Currently the organization has its headquarters at a spectacular retreat center in the high desert of Yucca Valley, California. Designed and built by Frank Lloyd Wright, the Mentalphysics' facilities are ideal for study and meditation. The surrounding San Jacinto and San Gorgonio mountain ranges emanate waves of energy which blanket the entire high-desert plateau.

The following breaths are among those learned and taught by Dingle, whose "spiritual" name was Ding Le Mei. I have changed the names of the breaths, deleted some breaths altogether, and present them here in an order which I believe best maximizes their power.

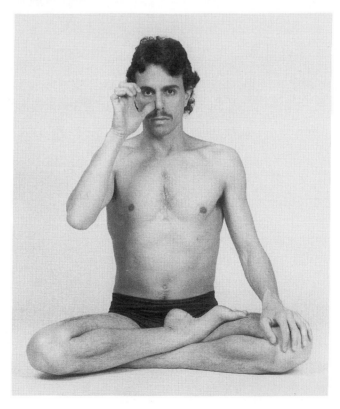

The Balancing Breath: Sit in a cross-legged position with the spine straight. Blocking your right nostril with your right thumb, inhale steadily through your left nostril to a count of four. Hold the breath to a count of sixteen. Then block off your left nostril with your left thumb, and exhale steadily through the right nostril to a count of eight. Now keep the left nostril blocked with your left thumb, and inhale steadily through the right nostril to a count of four. Perform this breath four times, twice inhaling through the left nostril, and twice inhaling through the right nostril.

The Balancing Breath balances the solar/lunar, positive/negative forces of the body-mind. It creates a balance of Yin and Yang by activating equally Ida and Pingala, the energy channels which run, from the left and right nostrils respectively, over the head and alongside the spinal column. Ida is Yin, lunar, negative, and Pingala is Yang, solar, positive. The Balancing Breath creates harmony within the body-mind. This breath can be practiced up to four times daily—upon rising, at noon, at dusk, and prior to retiring at night.

The Power Breath: Stand straight with your arms by your sides. Inhale deeply and completely, filling yourself with the breath to maximum capacity. Hold the breath for half a minute.

Then exhale powerfully through the mouth with your lips like a pipe. As you exhale, draw your lower abdomen in tightly, squeezing the breath out. When you have completed the exhalation, inhale lightly, exhale, and relax for a moment. This breath can be performed up to seven times.

The Power Breath supercharges the body-mind. It saturates your entire system with prana, the energy of the breath. It develops mental clarity, purifies the blood, and builds strong, powerful lungs.

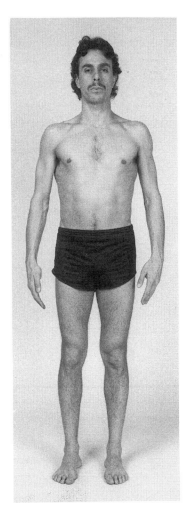

The Super Brain Breath: Sit cross-legged with your spine straight, or on a chair or stool with your spine straight. Place your hands on your thighs with the palms up. Your head is down, and your shoulders are relaxed. Inhaling through the nose, swing your head all the way back. The inhalation and motion are short and forceful. Then exhale quickly and forcefully through the teeth, swinging your head all the way forward, with your chin to your chest.

Repeat the breath and motion seven times, without pausing between breaths. When you have done this, take a long, deep breath and relax. This is the completion of one full round. This breath can be performed a maximum of seven rounds, or forty-nine breaths. Start practicing this breath for three rounds, or twenty-one breaths.

The Super Brain Breath charges the brain with energy, increases blood flow to the base of the brain, and increases the flow of *cerebrospinal fluid* (CSF). This breath is reputed to enhance memory, because of its stimulation of the *medulla*, which is at the base of the brain, and which is the center of memory function.

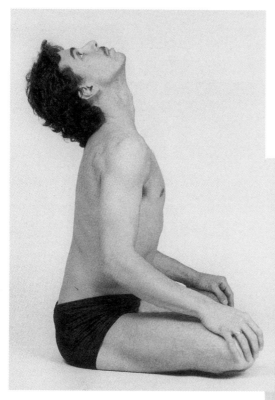
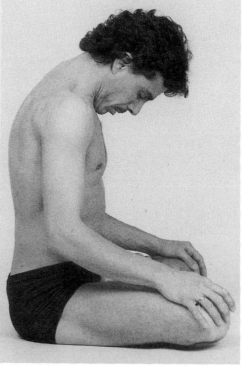

The Aura Builder

Stand perfectly straight with your arms by your sides. As you inhale deeply
through your nose, raise your arms straight out to the sides and then up above
your head, placing the backs of your hands together. Your arms should be
stretched up as high as possible. Hold the breath for several seconds. With your
lips like a pipe, exhale a quarter of the breath through the mouth, and lower the
arms to a 120-degree angle. Exhale another quarter of the breath, as you lower
the arms to a 90-degree angle. Exhale another quarter of the breath as you lower
the arms to a 45-degree angle. Exhale the last quarter of the breath as you lower
the arms to your sides.

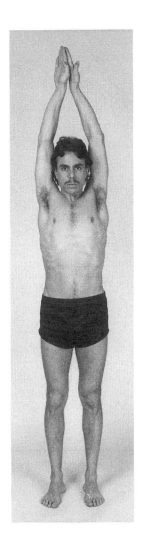

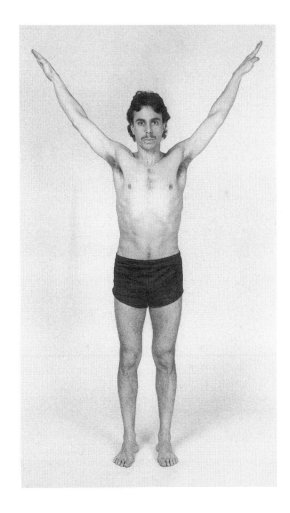

This breath can be performed a maximum of seven times. Start out practicing this breath just three times.

The Aura Builder expands and strengthens the aura, which is the energy field which surrounds and emanates from you. The aura acts as a protective and healing membrane. As the aura becomes brighter and stronger, it filters out psychic static and "vibratory pollution." At the same time, you become more keenly aware of the space around you, and more sensitive to subtle changes in your environment. A healthy, vibrant aura is an extension of a healthy, vibrant body-mind.

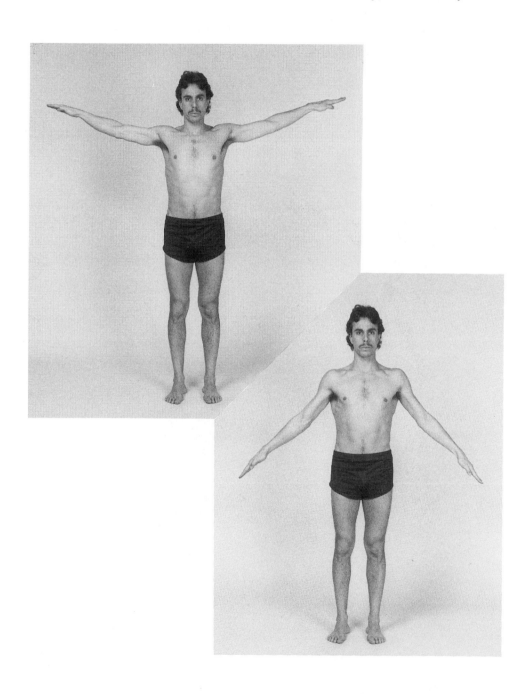

The Invincible Breath

Stand up straight with your feet several inches apart. Your arms are together, straight out in front of you, with the hands in fists. Take a full, deep breath through the nose, and hold it. Holding the breath, swing your arms straight back as far as they will go, and then swing them forward again. Repeat this three times. When you have done that, exhale through the mouth, with your lips like a pipe. Then bring your arms to your sides and rest for a moment. That completes one full breath.

This breath can be performed a maximum of seven times. Start out practicing it just three times.

This is known as the Invincible Breath because it stimulates the thymus gland, which lies in the center of the chest. The thymus is responsible for immunity to disease. Regular practice of this breath develops the immune system, and builds resistance to disease.

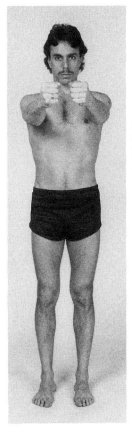
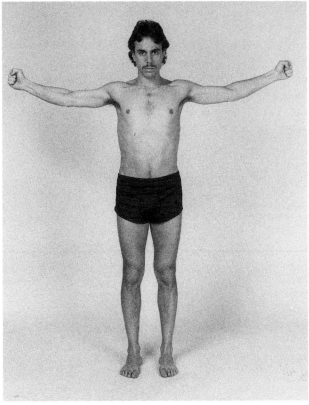

The Vibrational Breath

Stand straight, with your arms by your sides, and your feet several inches apart. Inhale fully and deeply through the nose, and hold the breath. Holding the breath, swing your arms up in a complete circle, three times. After completing the third swing, bring your arms back to your sides and exhale forcefully through the mouth. This completes one breath. This breath is performed for a maximum of seven times. Start out practicing this three times.

The Vibrational Breath attunes your senses to vibrations around you. It is also valuable for the heart and lungs.

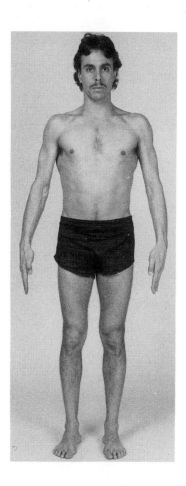
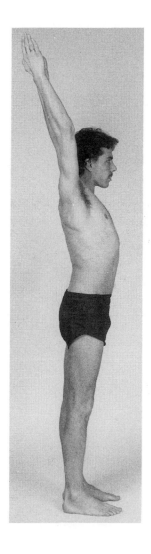

The Sun in the Heart ——

Sit either in full lotus position, or in a comfortable cross-legged position with your spine straight. Your arms are extended straight out in front of you, with your hands clenched in fists. In this position, exhale fully through the mouth.

Inhale slowly and deeply through the nose. As you do, pull your fists toward you. Visualize that you are drawing the sun into the center of your chest.

When you have completed the inhalation, your fists will be tucked close to your armpits. Hold the breath as long as you can comfortably, and continue to visualize the sun burning in the center of your chest. Holding this position, exhale fully through the mouth.

Relax your hands on your knees for a moment. This completes one full breath.

This breath is performed for a maximum of seven times. Start out practicing it three times.

The Sun In The Heart purifies the heart chakra, which is the center of love and compassion. This also acts on the thymus gland to enhance immunity to disease.

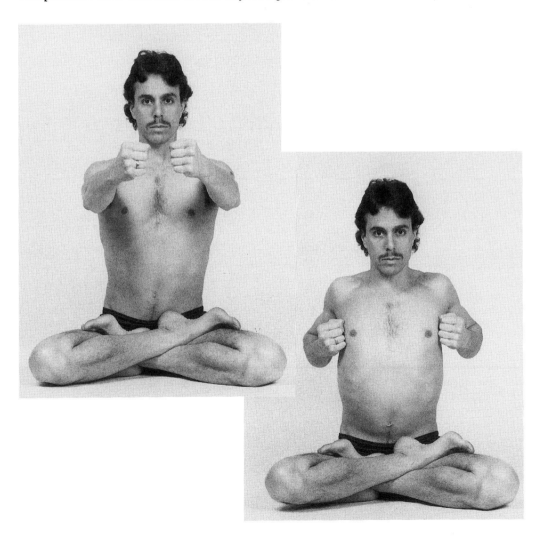

Initiate's Breath ———————————————————

Stand straight with your feet about shoulder's width apart, and your hands on your hips. In this position, take a long, full, deep breath through the nose, and hold it.

Holding the breath, bend as far to the right as you can, and then to the left. Repeat this three times without a break.

Then come up straight, and exhale forcefully through the mouth. This completes one full breath.

This breath is performed a maximum of seven times. Start out practicing this breath three times.

The Initiate's Breath stimulates lower spinal energy, and concentrates the force of the Kundalini Shakti at the base of the spine. This is one of the most powerful of all breaths. It is very useful for breaking up blockages in the human energy system.

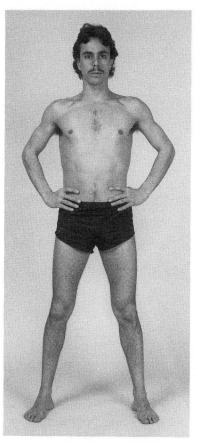

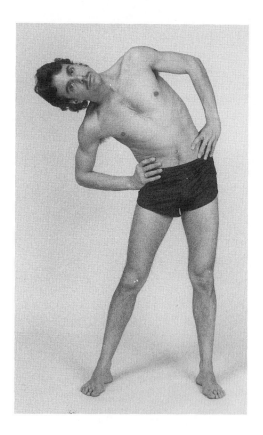

The Immortal Breath

Stand straight with your feet several inches apart, and your hands on your hips. In this position, take a full, deep breath through the nose. Holding the breath, tuck your chin into your chest, and then swing your head up and back. Repeat this three times, while holding the breath.

As you forcefully exhale through the mouth, bend as far forward as you can, and then as far back as possible. Repeat this three times.

Then come up straight, and inhale through your nose. Follow this with one normal breath. This completes one full round of the Immortal Breath.

The Immortal Breath is performed a maximum of seven times. Start out practicing this breath three times.

The Immortal Breath activates all the chakras, and stimulates the flow of Kundalini Shakti. This breath supercharges the entire glandular system, and is a superb health-builder.

The Shakti Breath

Sit either in full lotus position, or on the knees sitting back on the heels, or in a chair. Your spine should be very straight. Your hands are behind your head with your fingers interlocking, and your elbows straight out to the sides. In this position, inhale fully and deeply through the nose, and hold the breath.

Holding the breath, bend forward (bend from the hips), as far as you can. Hold this position to a count of seven.

Come up to the first position, and exhale through the mouth, with your lips like a pipe. This completes one full breath.

The Shakti Breath is performed for a maximum of seven times. Start out practicing this breath three times.

The Shakti Breath works directly on raising Kundalini energy up the spine. This particular method is very powerful, and is an excellent breath to practice prior to meditation.

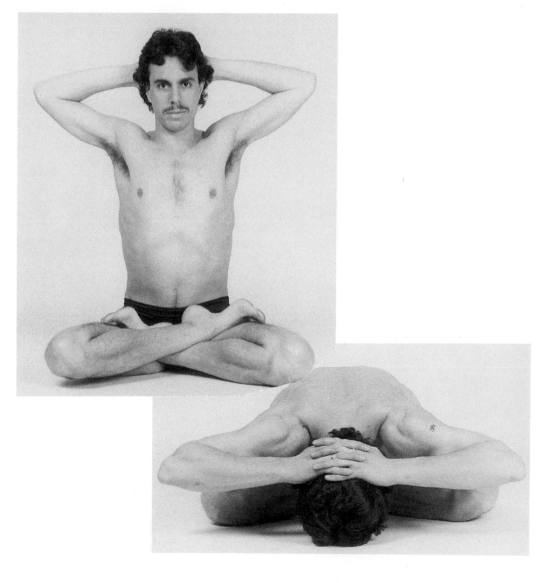

5. Chuang Fu

Chuang Fu is a series of exercises for flexibility, strength, and energy. These Tibetan yoga exercises are the warm-ups for Buddha Hands Kung Fu, an ancient martial art which originated in Tibet. While the Chinese term "kung fu" is inclusive of all martial arts, Buddha Hands is a particular style.

Buddha Hands is a mountain style of Kung Fu, developed in the treacherous terrain of the Tibetan mountains. The legend of Buddha Hands is that the fundamentals of the system were first taught over four thousand years ago by a Buddha —an enlightened sage, and that the style originated directly from God. While we may never know the actual origin of Buddha Hands, the style is old, simple, powerful, and utterly deadly. It is the ultimate combat art.

The monks who traveled the rigorous Tibetan terrain, itself hostile and unforgiving, needed protection from bandits and roving outlaws. For a fortunate few, Buddha Hands was a refuge, a sacred gift which transformed the monks into unrelenting fighting machines. A proficiency in this style enabled many monks to reach their destinations safely.

Today, Buddha Hands is little known. What few teachers there are can be found in China and Burma. The only Buddha Hands master in the West is Alex Anatolev, who teaches in Boston, Massachusetts. A direct student of grand master Lu Yang Tai, Alex Anatolev is currently the eminent teacher of this combat system. Alex provides instruction in Buddha Hands to a small but dedicated group of students six days a week.

The accomplished Buddha Hands martial artist is elemental and uncanny. Through the refinement that comes with thousands of hours of assiduous practice, he can move like the wind, flow like water, rage like fire, and strike like iron. The Buddha Hands adept develops his own animal nature to a high degree. As an animal, his senses are refined, and sensitivity to the environment becomes acute. By diligent practice, the body-mind is developed to function automatically, powerfully, and elegantly. All motion becomes instinctive and spontaneous, and a maximum effect is achieved with what appears to be a minimum of effort. In actuality, the martial artist cultivates the natural potential of the body-mind. The results of this careful cultivation seem to be superhuman, but they are not. The speed, power, agility, and deftness of the Buddha-Hands adept are in fact common in the animal world.

What distinguishes the Buddha-Hands adept from the rest of the animal kingdom is his ability to use the development of the body-mind as a spiritual method, a Way of total fulfillment. Such development cannot be realized through intellectual consideration or speculation. It occurs as an organic process, as one involves the body-mind in regular, rigorous practice.

The accomplished Buddha-Hands practitioner is a master of the unexpected. He is free from ritual and pre-determined patterns of behavior. He has assimilated the complex and made it simple. In combat, he is the most dangerous opponent. You never know where he is, or what he will do, and he works with blinding speed and overwhelming power.

The Chuang Fu exercises shown here are used in Buddha Hands Kung Fu prior to practice. Some of the exercises are similar to many popular Western methods of physical fitness. Some are quite different. Practiced daily, in sequence, they will strengthen, tone, stretch, and invigorate you, and greatly enhance Chi flow.

Horse Stance: Stand with your feet wider than shoulder's width apart. Your feet are parallel to each other, your knees are bent and wide apart. Your back is straight, with a small inward curve in the lower spine. Your shoulders are relaxed. Place your hands on your thighs, and breathe long and slow. In Horse Stance, always move slightly up to down, and side to side, rather than remaining in a rigid position. Hold Horse Stance for five to ten minutes.

Benefits: Horse Stance strengthens the lower body, legs, back, and abdomen. It also gently heats the body, concentrating energy in the lower abdomen. This position "opens the body up" for the rest of the Chuang Fu series.

Neck Rolls: Standing in Horse Stance, slowly roll the head on the neck in a counter-clockwise direction several times, then very quickly a few more turns. The eyes and mouth remain open as you move. Stop and breathe deeply several times. Then repeat the same motion in a clockwise direction.

Benefits: This exercise loosens, stretches, and strengthens the neck. It also develops the vestibular and oculomotor nerves, minimizing dizziness and improving visual stability during rapid head movements such as those which may be required in combat.

Hands Together, Elbows to Ground: Standing in Horse Stance, place your right fist in your left palm, and bend forward, touching your arms and elbows to the ground. Stretch up several inches, then down again, inhaling up, exhaling down. Repeat nine times.

Benefits: This exercise loosens the lower back, and opens up the crotch a little.

Stretch #1: Place your left foot flat on the ground, with your right fist planted parallel to it, about eighteen-inches apart. Your right leg is straight, with your right foot flat on the floor, perpendicular to your left. With your left arm bent at a ninety-degree angle, stretch down and touch the ground with the elbow, inhaling up and exhaling down. Repeat five times. Switch sides and repeat the same process.

Benefits: This exercise stretches and tones the inner thighs, crotch, and lower back.

Knife Defense Stretching: Stand with your feet about twice shoulder's width apart. The feet are parallel, your right knee is bent, and your left leg is straight. With your right arm bent so that your right hand is behind your right ear, stretch your left fist down your left leg, toward the left foot. Stretch like this five times. Switch sides and repeat the same thing.

Benefits: This exercise stretches the sides, crotch, legs and lower back.

Push-Ups on Palms: Interlock your fingers, and place your palms flat on the floor under your chest. In this position, do twenty-five push-ups, inhaling down and exhaling up, keeping your back completely straight.

Benefits: This exercise strengthens the arms, back, chest, and shoulders.

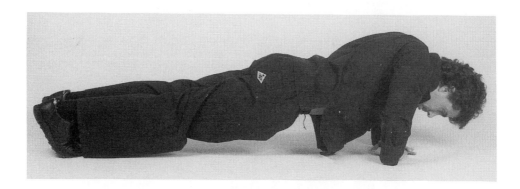

Stretch #2:   Place the knife-edge of your left foot on the floor, toes pointing straight ahead. Your fists are flat on the floor on each side of your foot. Your right leg is stretched out straight behind you, resting on the ball of your right foot. Stretch down and touch your nose to your toes. Push up a little bit, then stretch down, inhaling up, exhaling down. Repeat five times. Repeat the same steps on the other side.

Benefits: This exercise stretches and tones the hips, crotch, and lower back.

Legs Apart, Nose to Floor: Stand with your legs straight, feet wide apart, flat on the floor. With your hands behind your knees, bend forward and touch your nose to the floor, rising up slightly and then stretching down again, inhaling up, exhaling down. Repeat twenty-seven times.

Benefits: This exercise stretches and tones the lower back, the backs of the legs, the hips, and crotch.

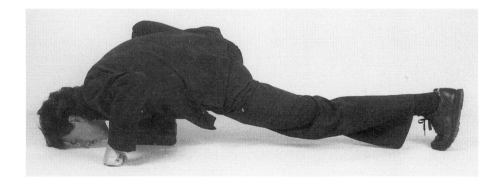

Double Kicks: Sitting on your tailbone, draw the knees tight to the chest, with the feet together and off the ground. Your hands are slightly in front of your knees. As you exhale slowly through the mouth, extend your legs straight out, tucking your chin into your chest, fists protecting your liver and heart. When you are fully extended, tense your entire body for a moment. Inhale as you come back up to the first position. Repeat this motion, keeping the feet off the floor, twenty-five times. The pace is moderate.

Benefits: This exercise tones and strengthens the abdomen, the upper thighs, hips, back, sides, and chest. This is an exceptional exercise, and its power should not be underestimated.

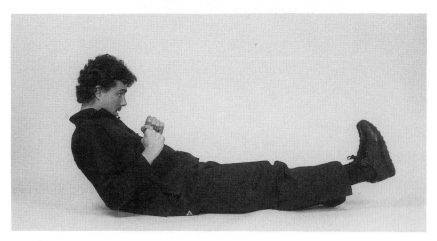

Push-Ups on Bear Claws: With the hands in Bear Claws (see photograph), do twenty-five push-ups on the flat part of your fists, between the first and second knuckles. Inhale down and exhale up. Keep your back perfectly straight.

Benefits: This exercise strengthens the arms, wrists, chest, shoulders, and back.

Chest to Knee Stretch: Your right leg is slightly bent, foot planted flat on the floor, pointing straightahead. Your left leg is straight, with the heel of your left foot resting on the floor and your toes pulled back, at a forty-five-degree angle to your right foot, about fifteen inches away. With your hands on your hips, bend down, touching your chest to your left knee. Come up a little, then stretch down again, inhaling up, exhaling down. Repeat five times. Switch sides and repeat the same steps.

Benefits: Strengthens the lower back, hips, thighs, and gluteal muscles.

Stretching for Straight Kick: Stand with your left leg bent in front, and your right leg stretched behind you. Your head and torso are straight, and your hands are on your hips. With your right leg, kick straight forward and up as high as you can, keeping your head and torso straight. Repeat this five times. Switch sides and repeat the same thing.

Benefits: This stretches the legs, and improves hip flexibility and balance.

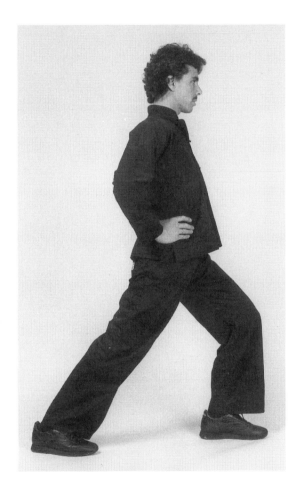

Stretching for Side Kick: Stand with the feet together and the knees bent. Your hands are on your hips. Keeping your head and torso straight, kick out to the side with your left leg, five times. Switch sides and repeat.

Benefits: This stretches the hips, and facilitates balance and stability.

Push-Ups on Two Knuckles: Make fists with your hands, and place the first two knuckles of each hand on the floor. Do twenty-five push-ups, inhaling down, exhaling up. Make sure you remain on just the first two knuckles, and keep your back perfectly straight.

Benefits: This exercise strengthens the hands, wrists, arms, chest, shoulders, and back.

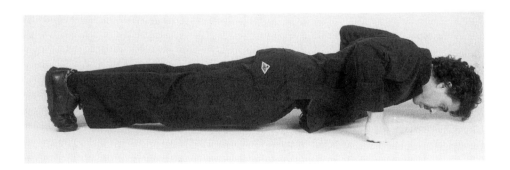

Practice the Chuang Fu Exercises Daily: After two weeks, your body will feel somewhat stronger. After two months, you will look and feel in better shape. After a year, your body will be much stronger, more flexible, and well-toned.

6. The Five Elements Exercises

The theory of the five elements, or Wu-Hsing, is a key to understanding the natural world. Believed to have been developed over two thousand years ago by Chinese sages, the Wu-Hsing integrates the human body-mind, nature, and the cosmos. The five elements themselves—wood, fire, earth, metal, and water—are not physical substances, but energetic processes, or permutations of Chi, the one unifying energy of all creation. Each element is representative of a planet, a season, a direction, a color, and so on. The theory of the five elements not only categorizes absolutely everything in the phenomenal universe, but describes the relationship(s) between all things.

The Wu-Hsing provides a basis for understanding the human body-mind, spirit, emotion, health, disease, diagnosis, treatment, diet, and all the subtleties of a human being. By explaining the relationship between man and nature, the Wu-Hsing is the foundation for various systems of hygiene, medicine, martial arts, and exercise. Each individual, according to the balance of the five elements within them, as well as the season, the climate, and the specific energy of the place in which they live, can use the principles of the five elements to achieve health, happiness, and longevity.

Before describing the five elements exercises, it is useful to give a brief explanation of the five elements. For a more thorough understanding of Wu-Hsing, I recommend that you read the *Yellow Emperor's Classic of Internal Medicine*. That treatise is the basis of Chinese medicine, diet, and acupuncture, and is a study guide for virtually all students of traditional Chinese systems, from medicine to the fighting arts.

There are four key principles which describe the relationship between the five elements:

1. *Mutual Creation*—The five elements create each other. Wood creates fire, fire creates earth, earth creates metal, metal creates water, and water creates wood.
2. *Mutual Closeness*—Each element is attracted to the element of its origin. Wood is close to water, water to metal, metal to earth, earth to fire, fire to wood.
3. *Mutual Destruction*—Each element can be weakened or destroyed by another. Wood destroys earth, earth destroys water, water destroys fire, fire destroys metal, and metal destroys wood.
4. *Mutual Fear*—Each element fears that element which can destroy it. Wood fears metal, metal fears fire, fire fears water, water fears earth, and earth fears wood.

The following is an assortment of "factors" for which a concordance has been established with the five elements. For purposes of convenience, I have grouped these factors together in the following categories: cosmic factors, natural factors, human factors, sensory factors and dietary factors.

The information in these categories has been checked against several sources. There are three categories, however, for which I cannot guarantee certainty. The first is that of musical notes. While all sources gave the same Chinese names for the notes listed here, I could find no translation for what the notes are. Is *Kung* a High C? Perhaps a Chinese scholar can answer that.

Cosmic Factors	WOOD	FIRE	EARTH	METAL	WATER
Direction	East	South	Center	West	North
Planet	Jupiter	Mars	Saturn	Venus	Mercury
Color	Green	Red	Yellow	White	Black
Number	8	7	5	9	6
Musical Note	*Chio*	*Chih*	*Kung*	*Shang*	*Yu*

Natural Factors

			Long Summer		
Season	Spring	Summer	Late Summer	Fall	Winter
Injurious Climate	Wind	Heat	Humidity	Dryness	Cold
Development	Birth	Growth	Transformation	Harvest	Store

Human Factors

				Animal	
Spiritual Resources	Soul	Spirit	Ideas	Spirit	Will
Emotion	Anger	Joy	Sympathy	Grief	Fear
Expression	Shout	Laugh	Sing	Weep	Groan
Senses	Sight	Taste	Touch	Smell	Hearing
Yin Organs (Viscera)	Liver	Heart	Spleen	Lungs	Kidneys
Yang Organs (Bowels)	Gall Bladder	Small Intestine	Stomach	Large Intestine	Bladder
Orifices	Eyes	Ears	Nose	Mouth	Lower Orifices
Tissues	Ligaments	Arteries	Muscles	Skin/Hair	Bones
Secretions	Tears	Sweat	Saliva	Mucus	Urine

Sensory Factors

Odor	Rancid	Scorched	Fragrant	Rotten	Putrid
Flavor	Sour	Bitter	Sweet	Pungent	Salty

Dietary Factors

Five Grains	Wheat	Corn	Millet	Rice	Beans
Five Tree Fruits	Peaches	Plums	Apricots	Chestnuts	Dates
Five Meats	Foul	Mutton	Beef	Horse	Pork
Five Vegetables	Mallows	Coarse Greens	Scallions	Onions	Leeks

Three sources disagree on the category of secretions. Two associated urine with the element water, while another lists spittle there instead. Lastly, there is widespread disagreement regarding the category of vegetables. I have made choices which seem the most reasonable.

These minor discrepancies aside, the following information gives some insight into the complex interactions between several realms of factors, as discerned by the ancient Chinese sages.

A person who can balance the five elements within the body-mind can achieve harmony. This harmony translates into enduring health, vitality, and long life. The following exercises are known as the Five Elements Exercises. Each exercise is related to one of the five elements. Together, these exercises are meant to balance the elements within the body-mind.

The Five Elements Exercises should be practiced daily, on an empty stomach. Morning is an ideal time to practice, though they can be repeated in the evening.

The Five Elements Exercises combine the breath, motion, posture, and concentration of attention. Each exercise activates the energy circuits, or meridians. This activation stimulates Chi-flow throughout the entire body-mind.

Five Elements Exercise #1:   Sit on your knees, sitting back on the heels. Your hands are in your lap, fingers interlocking, thumb tips touching, and palms up.

Inhale deeply through the nose, filling your lungs completely. As you do this, raise your hands to the level of your throat, and concentrate on vital energy filling you along with the breath.

Turning your hands over, push your palms upward toward the sky as you exhale out the mouth with your lips like a pipe.

Inhale deeply through the nose once more, bringing your hands to the top of your head.

Then exhale, lowering your hands to your lap.

Perform this exercise nine times, without interruption.

Five Elements Exercise #2:   Sit on your knees sitting back on the heels. Your hands are resting on your knees.

As you inhale deeply through the nose, raise your arms, with the hands hanging loosely at the wrists.

Then exhale out the mouth, lowering your hands to the first position.

Perform this exercise nine times without interruption.

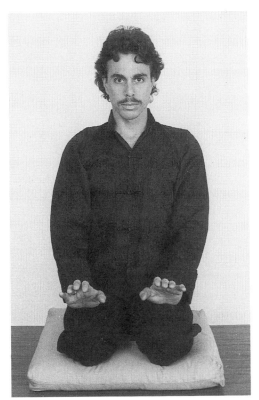

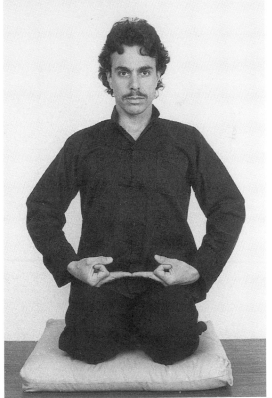

Five Elements Exercise #3: Sit on your knees sitting back on the heels. Your mouth is closed, teeth together, and tongue lightly touching the upper palate.

Your hands are in your lap, index fingers curled in on themselves, thumbs pressing down on the index fingers, palms facing up.

In this position, inhale slowly and steadily through the nose. As you do, mentally draw energy from the very base of your spine, up along the spine to the top of your head.

As you exhale through the nose, circulate that energy from the top of your head down, along the middle of the front of your body, all the way to the base of the spine.

Perform this exercise seven times, without interruption.

Five Elements Exercise 4: Sit on your knees, sitting back on the heels. Your arms form a circle in front of you, with the finger tips pointing toward each other.

Inhale deeply through the nose. As you do, mentally draw energy through the finger tips of your right hand, through your right arm, into your chest. As you exhale through the mouth, continue to circulate the energy out your left arm, and out the finger tips of your left hand.

Perform this exercise three times without interruption.

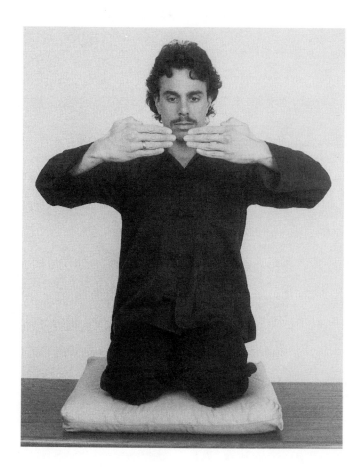

Five Elements Exercise #5:   Sit on your knees, sitting back on the heels. Your arms are by your sides. Inhale deeply through the nose, raising your arms out to the sides with the palms of your hands facing downward, and continue until your arms are above your head.

As you exhale half the breath through the mouth, bring your hands down to throat level as though you are pulling down a beam of energy. Holding half the breath, look into the space between the hands, as though you could see the energy. (Eventually you will.)

As you need to, complete the exhalation, bringing your hands down to the first position.

Perform this exercise nine times without interruption.

7. The Five Tibetans

The Himalayan region between India and China is some of the wildest, least accessible, and most treacherous terrain on earth. An individual could spend a lifetime exploring the thousands of foothills, rivers, gorges, canyons, and sheer peaks which make up this remote area, called "the roof of the world." Not only is this region remote, but it is sparsely populated. There are areas where the climate is so harsh, or the altitude so high, that very few people ever venture there. In addition, there is little pollution, and much fresh, brisk air, and clean water.

Nestled among the peaks and rivers, there are secluded ashrams, monasteries, retreats, and sacred sites where Yogis, sages, and wanderers live, meditate, study, and pursue the awakening of Shakti powers. Many of these holy places are small, inhabited by one or two people. But others are large communities, with housing, gardens, temples, schools, and cottage industries. In such communities, the awakening of the spiritual self is the hub around which all life revolves.

Life in the spiritual communities of the Himalayan region is almost always simple. While there is electricity in some of these centers, the majority of them are lit by fire and candles. Hot water for bathing is unknown. While practices vary greatly from one place to another, schedules are usually similar. Rising time is usually well before dawn, around three or four in the morning. After bathing (in a river, stream, or other body of water), there will be chanting, meditation, singing, group prayer, and exercise. Many communities postpone breakfast until late morning, after a work period. In one remote temple that I visited, only one meal per day was served—a frugal one at that!

Work is important to any community, and it is no less so for those which are spiritually oriented. Often referred to as *Karma* Yoga, work is performed as a selfless sacrifice, and the fruits of one's labors are dedicated to God, Buddha, or whatever deity may be associated with the community and its teachings. Meals are usually taken together, often in silence. Evenings are almost always filled with study, meditation, and more group practices. Often at this time the head of the community, the guru or chief teacher, will give discourse, explaining the subtleties of the spiritual path. This time is a bonding period for the whole community.

In most spiritual communities, the guru or main teacher is the center of activity. Each member of the group will engage in specific practices, usually given by the teacher. Thus individuals at all levels of development are accommodated in their pursuit of personal integration. The guru or teacher is the final authority in such groups, and the other members turn to that individual, male or female, for guidance and counsel. Often the teacher is regarded as the actual embodiment of a particular god or power, and is highly revered. In almost all instances, the leader of a spiritual community is treated with great care and consideration. The Eastern mentality is quite different from that of the West in this regard. In the West, such reverence is virtually unknown. With the exception of the Pope and a handful of transplanted Eastern guru's, very few individuals in the Occidental world are treated as specially as the spiritual leaders in the East. Neither the Eastern nor Western manner is better, but the difference is significant.

Up until the 1950s, there were many Tibetan monasteries, with populations of several thousand aspirants. In fact, of all the nations in the world, Tibet had the most extensive monastic population. It was both common and desirable for a child to be accepted as part of a monastery. Monastic life afforded both a respected place in society and a home for life. But when China invaded Tibet, the spiritual communities were dispersed, dismantled, and destroyed. Sacred sites were desecrated, and the inhabitants tortured and killed. Tens of thousands of scriptures and sacred writings were ruined and burned, and every effort was made to eradicate sacred and religious practices from the Tibetan culture. The systematic genocide of the Tibetan people, and their subsequent "re-acculturation" is one of the saddest and most pathetic chapters in human history.

Fortunately for humanity, however, many sacred Tibetan teachings were preserved and guarded by those who fled the Chinese purge. These teachings include methods of meditation, medicine, and martial arts, which were developed over thousands of years. Among these are the Five Tibetans, a unique set of five simple physical exercises. In the monastery from which they originate, the Five Tibetans were performed twice daily by the entire community. These exercises, while relatively easy to perform, are profound for renewing the vital life-force of the body-mind. The "Tibetans" inhibit the aging process, and endow the practitioner with boundless vitality. In fact, they were used by Lamas (Buddhist monks) as a fountain of youth.

The Five Tibetans stimulate the chakras and their corresponding nerve plexuses and glands. By balancing the psychic energies of the body-mind, they promote a strong immune defense system, maintain keenly developed nerve transmission, and establish a balanced hormonal climate. They tone and stretch major muscle groups, creating a strong, flexible physique. They take only about five minutes to perform, yet are a complete and sophisticated yogic system. I have never encountered anything quite like them. At the time of this writing, I have practiced the Five Tibetans daily for ten years. In my opinion, they are without par.

The morning is the best time to practice this series. At that time, you supercharge the entire body-mind, so that it is impregnated with vital force. This energy will circulate through you all day long, empowering you in everything you do. The Five Tibetans can also be practiced again at night, before retiring. If you do this, you will sleep deeply and awaken refreshed.

The Five Tibetans are practiced twenty-one times each. Most people need to work up to this number of repetitions, starting out with ten or twelve each. In fact, almost everyone who practices these exercises works up to the maximum number over a month or two. Do not be concerned with doing the full number at first. Take your time, and as you go along the Tibetans will begin to work on you. As vital force flows more strongly through you, you will notice changes in the way you feel. Interestingly enough, there is no need to exceed twenty-one repetitions for each of the Tibetans. That number is exactly correct to derive maximum benefit from this unique routine.

Please refer to the photographs accompanying each exercise to get the position right.

Tibetan Exercise #1:   Stand up straight, with the arms outstretched to the sides. The fingers are together, palms open and down. Now spin in a full circle in a clockwise direction. Repeat the spin twenty-one times without a break. When you are done, stand with the hands on the hips and take two long, deep breaths, exhaling through the mouth. Take two breaths in this manner after each of the Tibetans.

Please note that the direction in which you spin is clockwise. If you were to turn your head to the right, you would spin in that right direction. You may experience some dizziness when you first start to practice this. Do not do too much too quickly. With regular practice, the dizziness will stop and the motion will be easy, even at high speeds.

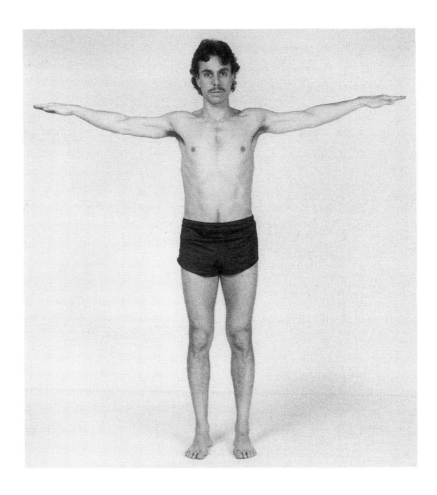

Tibetan Exercise #2: Lie on your back on a mat or rug. The legs are together and out straight, and the arms are by the sides with the palms flat on the floor. As you inhale, raise the legs up straight. The toes will be pointing toward the ceiling, but the lower back remains flat on the ground. As you bring the legs up, the head comes up also, with the chin tucked against the chest. This is all done in one smooth motion.

As you exhale, bring the legs and head down to the first position, with the body supine. Repeat the entire motion twenty-one times, inhaling as you bring the legs and head up, and exhaling as they come down.

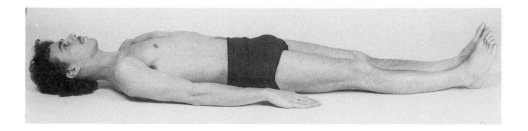

Tibetan Exercise #3:   Stand up on the knees. Your legs will be behind you, and the balls of the feet should be pressed on the floor. The knees are about four-inches apart. The hands are placed with the palms flat against the backs of the thighs, just below the buttocks. The chin is tucked into the chest, though you are standing straight.

Inhale, and as you do, arch back from the waist, dropping the head back as far as it will go. Your hands will support you as you lean back. Then exhale, returning up and forward to the first position. Repeat the entire motion twenty-one times in a steady, unbroken rhythm.

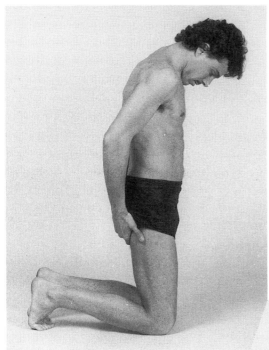

Tibetan Exercise #4: Sit up straight with the legs together and outstretched in front of you. The chin is tucked into the chest, and the arms are straight by the sides, with the palms flat against the floor beside your hips. Placement of the hands is particularly important; they should be exactly beside the hips.

Inhale and raise the hips, bending the knees up, bringing the soles of the feet flat to the floor. You will come into a position in which the body is parallel to the floor while the arms and legs are in a vertical position. The head is dropped all the way back. Then exhale and come back down to the original position.

Repeat the motion twenty-one times in a steady rhythm. Please note that in this exercise the feet do not slide; they stay in the same place. The arms do not bend at all; you merely pivot on the shoulders.

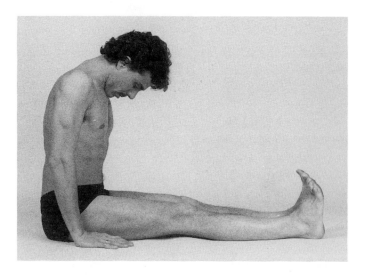

Tibetan Exercise #5: Start out on the hands and the balls of the feet, as though preparing to do push-ups. The hands are about two feet apart, as are the feet. Keeping the arms and legs perfectly straight, inhale as you raise the buttocks toward the sky, bringing your body into a perfect triangle. The chin is tucked into the chest in this position. Then exhale down to the starting position, with the head back as you sag down.

Your body should be off the ground or just barely touching. Repeat the entire motion twenty-one times, and then rest on your back for several minutes.

The Five Tibetans come from a monastic community, the members of which were celibate. This is typical for Eastern spiritual communities, and for monasteries and abbeys of Western Christian tradition as well. Many religions and spiritual traditions regard sexual activity as a distraction from spiritual life. Monks and nuns are required to live without sex. As you can well imagine, this can be an enormously frustrating way to live. In fact, it is so frustrating, that many monks and nuns do in fact engage in clandestine sex (with members of their own sex).

Beyond the belief that sex is a spiritual distraction (a notion which I believe is insane), many spiritual traditions teach that ejaculation during sexual intercourse depletes one's vitality. While ejaculation typically refers to a man's expression of semen, it can also refer to a woman's discharge of sexual fluids as well. Sexual fluids are considered to be supercharged with vital energy—energy which is lost upon ejaculation. To prevent loss of precious vitality, which leads to premature aging, the Tibetans developed a companion method to the Five Tibetans. You could call it the Sixth Tibetan.

The Sixth Tibetan is for those who wish to avoid frustration during sexual abstinence, or for those who are sexually active but choose not to ejaculate. This method is for the transmutation of sexual energy. It is for channeling sexual energy up the spine, from the lower chakras to the higher ones, to infuse the entire body-mind with vitality. If you are celibate, this method will enable you to deal more effectively with accumulated energy, and to relieve tension. If you are sexually active, this method will enable you to try a different kind of sexual intercourse. By refraining from ejaculation, sexual activity can be greatly prolonged, while still exquisitely pleasurable. Rather than having one specific orgasm, that same peak sexual pleasure can be spread out over a much longer period of time. By engaging in sex this way, sexual partners increase each other's energies. It is really like being plugged into a vitality generator. This method of intercourse enhances meditation, and can decrease your need for sleep. For a much longer, more detailed explanation of sexual traditions and practices, see my book *Stalking The Wild Orgasm*.

Tibetan Exercise #6: Stand up straight with the hands on the hips. The feet are about four inches apart. In this position, take a long, deep breath. Then exhale, and as you do, bend forward, leaning on the knees with your hands.

In this position, squeeze out all the breath, so that the abdomen is pulled in tightly. Then, while holding the breath out, come back up to a standing position, with the hands on the hips. In this position, with the abdomen pulled in tightly, hold your breath out for as long as is comfortable. Then take a deep breath and relax.

Repeat this technique a maximum of three times. Finish with two deep breaths with the hands on the *hips*, as with the other five Tibetans. Then relax on your back for several minutes.

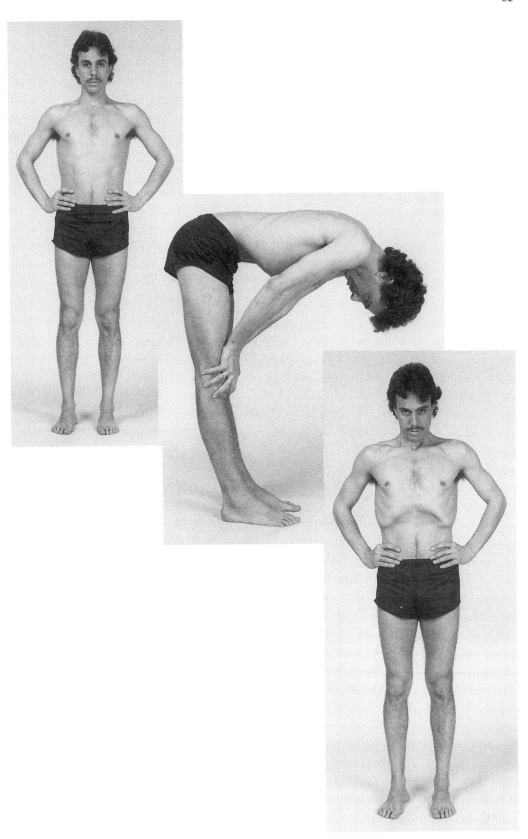

8. Kundalini Yoga

As described in the chapter on the Human Energy System, Kundalini is the power which lies at the base of the spine. It is said to be the principal evolutionary force, and the seat of genius and creativity in all humans. While it is not possible to defend or refute that position here, it is certain that there is an extraordinary psycho-biological force at the base of the spine. When this force is aroused, people do become more energetic, and often display what could be called supernatural powers. That is, the arousal of Kundalini energy presages a variety of extraordinary talents, including clairvoyance, extreme physical strength, amazing healing powers, and an assortment of other para-normal phenomena.

While the arousal of Kundalini, or of a similar force by other names, is common to virtually all cultures, the actual science of Kundalini Yoga itself originated in India, and has spread from there. Most often, the arousal of Kundalini energy happens suddenly, unexpectedly, and spontaneously. Such an occurrence can cause major upheaval in a person's life. Kundalini is so extremely potent that if it is aroused spontaneously, a person may experience severe drug-like states of mind, and a loss of physical and mental control. Kundalini-induced psychosis is becoming more widely known in the West, and is currently being investigated. Kundalini Yoga, however, is a systematic approach to the arousal of Kundalini. In this yoga, the entire body-mind is prepared for a greater flow of the force at the base of the spine. In the event of a full arousal of Kundalini, the practitioner is better prepared to handle the experience than a person who is untrained.

Over the course of thousands of years, the Yogis of India, especially those of the Himalayas, experimented with whole systems of yoga postures, breathing (pranayam), *mantra* (repetition of "sacred" sounds), and other methods. In their experimentation, they discovered a select variety of methods which seemed to quicken the process of awakening the Kundalini energy, which is typically represented as a serpent. Over time, these methods were assembled to form the science of Kundalini Yoga. This science has many forms—it is not limited to one small group of methods. Yet common to all the bona fide systems of Kundalini Yoga is the rapid development of the human energy system, and the intent to arouse Kundalini.

In fact, the awakening of Kundalini is the end result of all successful yoga practice. For this reason, it can be argued that all yoga is Kundalini Yoga. There is truth to this. However, the major systems of yoga currently in practice do not emphasize Kundalini arousal. If anything, they tend to downplay that eventuality, and in any case, take a long time to achieve that result. *Hatha* Yoga, for example, includes as many as several hundred yoga postures, plus breathing and meditation. An accomplished Hatha Yogi may possibly arouse Kundalini within a lifetime of practice. By comparison, practice of Kundalini Yoga can lead to that result within as little as a decade.

Kundalini is no joke. There are those who arouse Kundalini and go crazy. If you practice carefully and sanely, however, you should encounter no serious difficulties. **BUT** do not practice any of these methods under the influence of drugs. The effect can be utterly devastating, and may scare you away from practice for life.

If Kundalini is so powerful and potentially difficult to handle, why would anyone want to play with it at all? The answer to that question is very simple. Kundalini arousal can be one of the most exquisite, ecstatic experiences in life. A sexual orgasm pales by comparison. When the Kundalini force begins to flow up the spine, all senses are enlivened beyond what most people have ever known. A sense of sheer, unbridled ecstasy and unreasonable happiness completely overcomes you. It is as though all time has stopped, and you are on top of the world, dazzling, radiant, bathed in total joy. At the same time, there is profound peace, a lifting of all the burdens of life. When Kundalini has arisen, one dwells between pleasure and pain, timeless, without concern or worry.

Many people consider that such a condition is well worth attaining. As far as I can determine, such a way of being is not a goal—not something that one "goes after"—but is actually the true human condition. This is to say that sheer ecstasy is not a rare possibility, but an actual, fundamental condition of being. However, due to our upbringing and education, social conditions and demands, our attention is led away from such a way of being. Any true spiritual practice, then, does not actually create something new, but instead strips away layers of ignorance, pain, confusion, and misunderstanding, until unreasonable joy and happiness remain.

Thought of in this manner, Kundalini Yoga is a means of cleaning out the body-mind quickly and powerfully, of removing blockages in the energy system, of concentrating power at the base of the spine, and forcing Kundalini energy up through the entire chakra system. When this occurs, remaining dross is burned away at a rapid rate. The Kundalini force rapidly infuses the entire body-mind. Awareness is greatly enhanced, energy is increased, and life is changed forever.

Unfortunately, there are many bogus systems of Kundalini Yoga. In the United States, there are many teachers who claim to teach a complete Kundalini system. Be very wary. I personally have encountered only a few legitimate Kundalini Yogis. They were relatively unknown, fairly reclusive, and had only a small group of students. Beware of flash and funk and big promises. Promises are cheap to make, and people never run out of them. If a teacher tells you he can guarantee you enlightenment, or makes similar fantastic claims, walk away.

The methods of Kundalini Yoga which follow do not constitute a thorough and complete Kundalini practice. This is intentional. Such thorough practice is best learned directly from a teacher, not a book. However, if you diligently practice the following methods, you will get some very good results over time. Practiced in conjunction with other methods in this book, especially the Tibetan Breaths, these Kundalini techniques will make a very solid practice.

If you are a thrill-seeker and expect fantastic results in two weeks, do not bother to practice. Instead, try hang gliding off tall mountains, wrestling with alligators, and racing fast cars. Each of those will give you a thrill fast. Kundalini practice can actually do more for you, but it will alter you in the process. If you really want to practice, try to practice at the same time each day, and make sure that you do practice daily. Kundalini arousal is not like sculpting a stone. You can not pick up a hammer and chisel periodically and chip away at the piece of work. You are a living, ongoing process. So is the practice of Kundalini Yoga. By daily practice, you develop a rhythm, and you allow for certain alchemical changes to occur within you.

Kundalini practice will purify your system. You may notice changes in appetite, sleeping habits, sexual habits, dreams, and interests. You may find yourself more "awake" than before, and may experience enhanced mental function. Just keep practicing. You may even have fantastic experiences, such as traveling out of your body, seeing fantastic scenes in meditation, and knowing things before they occur. It is no big deal. Just keep practicing.

The spine is key to Kundalini practice. If you are a creature of poor posture, correct that. Get used to sitting up straight, and standing tall. The spine should be kept warm in cool weather. And you should keep yourself loose and flexible. If you practice the other methods in this book, especially the Chuang Fu exercises of Buddha Hands Kung Fu, and the Five Tibetans, you will be all set as far as strength and flexibility are concerned.

Also, make sure that you practice on an empty stomach, and that you wear loose, comfortable clothing (or nothing at all) when you practice. The cultivation of power is an art. If you are going to go about it, go about it skillfully and with great care. Now, on to Kundalini Yoga.

Spinal Twists

Sit in a comfortable cross-legged position, with your spine straight and your hands
on your knees. In this position, inhale lightly through the nose. As you exhale
through the mouth, twise your spine all the way to the left. You can use your
hands for leverage to twist further. Inhale lightly as you move back to the center,
then exhale again, this time twisting to the right.

Repeat this forty or more times on each side. Then, come to the center, take a
long, deep breath, hold it for as long as you can comfortably, then exhale and
relax for several minutes.

Explanation: Spinal Twists stimulate the lower spine with motion and breath.
The twisting action energizes Ida, Pingala, and Sushumna, the three major psychic
nerves of the spine. Breathing into any motion creates a much stronger charge than
just the motion itself. The deep breath and retention at the end are very important,
because it is when the breath is suspended that energy travels from the two side
channels of the spine (Ida and Pingala) to the central channel (Sushumna). It is at
that moment that Kundalini energy is most likely aroused.

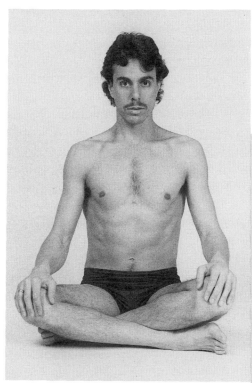
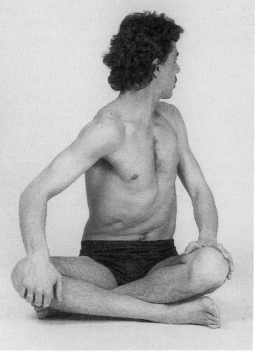

Siddhasan

Sit with your left heel tucked into your perineum, the spot directly between the anus and the genitals. Your right foot is tucked on top of the left. Your left heel should be pressed right into the perineum. Your spine is straight, and your hands are on your knees. Your chin is pulled in slightly, your mouth is closed with your front teeth together, and the tip of your tongue is pressed against your upper palate. The eyes are closed, and concentration is at the "third eye," the spot between the eyebrows, at the root of the nose.

In this position, inhale slowly and deeply through the nose, hold the breath as long as you can comfortably, then exhale through the nose. Continue this breathing for five minutes or more, then relax.

Explanation: Siddhasan is a powerful posture, because pressure is applied directly to the root chakra, Muladhara, which is the site of the Kundalini energy. When you couple this pressure with a straight spine, steady breathing, and concentration at the third eye, you complete a variety of important energy circuits, and create an optimal condition for Kundalini arousal. Siddhasan is an ideal position for deep meditation. You can actually practice this for an hour or more, eventually.

Lotus Pose ───────────────────────────────

Sitting upright, tuck the outer edge of your left foot into the crease of your right hip and inner thigh. Pull your right foot up over your left leg, tucking the outer edge of your right foot into the crease of your left hip and inner thigh. The hands are resting on the knees, with the thumbs and forefingers touching. Your spine is straight, and your breath is normal and even. Initially, try to maintain Lotus Pose for a few minutes. Eventually you can hold this posture for hours at a time, if you choose. This is the ideal pose for meditation.

Explanation: Lotus Pose completes a variety of energy circuits. It allows for smooth, steady energy flow, and it naturally causes Kundalini energy to rise. This pose is ideal for relieving pain, especially of a chronic nature. For meditation, it has no rival. If you can be comfortable in Lotus Pose (you can), then use it exclusively for meditation.

Lotus Alternate Knee Breathing

Sit in Lotus Pose, as described previously, but with your hands behind your back, with your right hand grabbing your left wrist.

In this position, inhale deeply through the nose. Then exhale through the mouth, and as you do, stretch down over your left leg, touching your left knee with your nose. Inhale up, and exhale down onto the right side. Repeat this at least forty times on each side.

Then come up straight, inhale deeply, and hold the breath for as long as you comfortably can. Then exhale and relax.

Explanation: Lotus Alternate Knee Breathing combines the power of Lotus Pose with the added charge of breath and motion. As with Spinal Twists, the action of this method stimulates the major energy channels of your spine. This is one of the most direct methods of Kundalini arousal.

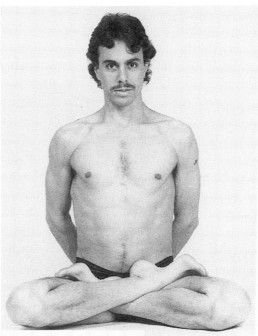

Cat Stretch ————————————————————————————————

Kneel on your hands and knees, with the insteps of your feet flat on the ground. As you inhale through the nose, stretch your head as far up and back as you can, while at the same time dropping your spine down. As you exhale through the mouth with your lips like a pipe, tuck your chin into your chest while you arch your spine up as high as you can. Repeat this forty or more times in a steady rhythm. At the end, take a long, deep breath, hold it as long as you can comfortably, then exhale and relax in a comfortable sitting position.

Explanation: The Cat Stretch charges the entire spinal column with energy. It also stimulates the flow of CSF, or cerebrospinal fluid. This fluid nourishes the brain. Cat Stretch awakens all the chakras, and clears away subtle blockages that lie along the spinal energy channels.

Mahamudra

Sit on the ground and extend your right leg in front of you. Tuck your left heel into your crotch, and hold the big toe of your right foot with both hands. Your spine is straight, with your chin tucked into your chest. In this position, inhale deeply through the nose, and hold the breath for a count of ten. Then exhale completely through the mouth, squeezing the last bit of breath out. Repeat this ten or more times on each side. Then relax for several minutes.

Explanation: *Mahamudra* applies dynamic tension to the spine and chakra system. In this position, the power of the breath acts as kindling for the fire of the Kundalini energy. Mahamudra is also revered as one of the greatest health-bestowing practices of all the yoga systems. It is excellent for digestion and for strengthening the immune system.

96

Reverse Seal

Lie on your back with your legs straight. Raise your legs, as though you were going to stretch them behind you. Supporting your hips with your hands, straighten your legs until they are exactly perpendicular to the ground. In this position, take a long, deep breath through the nose, and hold it to a count of ten. Exhale through the mouth. Repeat this breath ten times. Then relax for several minutes.

Explanation: Reverse Seal floods the brain with cerebrospinal fluid, and enriches the brain with energy. This posture is at the very core of classical Kundalini Yoga. It greatly increases Kundalini flow, and is reputed to transmute sexual energy into a more refined force which enhances meditation.

Yoga Mudra

Get into Lotus Pose. Once in this position, grasp your left wrist, from behind, with your right hand. Bend forward, touching the ground with your forehead.

In this position, breathe long and slowly, inhaling through the nose, and exhaling through either the nose or mouth. Continue for three minutes or longer. You can do this for an extended period of time—as long as thirty minutes.

Explanation: Yoga Mudra has all of the benefits of Lotus Pose, with an added pressure to the lower chakras. This pressure, coupled with the breath, concentrates a tremendous amount of energy around the site of the Kundalini energy. Yoga Mudra also increases blood flow to the brain, and directly stimulates the higher chakras.

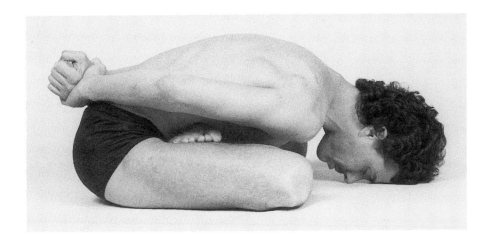

Yoni Mudra ————————————————————————————

Sitting either in Lotus Pose or in another cross-legged position, close your ears with your thumbs, your eyes with your index fingers, your nostrils with your middle fingers, your upper lips with your ring fingers, and your lower lips with your little fingers. When you need to breathe, open your nostrils and breathe. Hold the breath in as long as you can comfortably. Exhale through the nose. Focus your attention at the third eye throughout this practice. Hold this mudra for at least three minutes, or as long as you like.

Explanation: *Yoni* Mudra concentrates energy into the higher chakras. During practice, it is quite common to experience loud noises, vivid colors, and unusual visual effects. This method is described in detail in the *Vigyana Bhairava Tantra*, where it is presented as one of the 108 methods of enlightenment. In any case, Yoni Mudra is very powerful, and you will be surprised and delighted by regular practice of this strange method.

More on Kundalini

While the arousal of Kundalini is a specific process, each of us has some flow of Kundalini energy at all times. As a fundamental life-force, Kundalini is in fact active to some (small) extent in everyone. Also, most people have at one time or another, or perhaps at many times, those moments when the flow of this force is increased. For the average person, an enhanced flow of Kundalini energy is likely to occur during sex, at the moment of orgasm. The experience of being shot into space, of the loosening of the ties of the body, coupled with a sense of ecstasy, is a sexual experience which has some Kundalini involvement. Also, there are occasional moments of profound reverie which occur, when the world seems magnificent, complete, exquisite. It is at moments like these that there is often enhanced Kundalini flow.

Think of Kundalini as something akin to electricity. For most people, the Kundalini force which flows within is equal to the output of a pair of flashlight batteries. The actual potential charge of this force, however, is like the output of the power station at the Hoover Dam. It is enormous, beyond one's wildest imagining. If you try to run that kind of power through a flashlight, you will fry the flashlight in a second. If you suddenly were to unleash the full flow of Kundalini through the average untrained body-mind, that human being would be physically and mentally destroyed.

However, as I previously stated, with training you can develop a capacity to accept an ever greater flow of this enormous power. Through the practice of breathing techniques, the strengthening and cleansing of the body, and the training of the mind, you can safely channel a greater flow of Kundalini energy through you. When you regularly practice the methods in this book, for example, you accomplish all of the above, and you open the chakras up more each day. The chakras and their related energy pathways slowly and steadily become increasingly activated. As this occurs, more Kundalini force flows through the entire body-mind.

As the flow of Kundalini is stepped up, certain things happen. You will feel stronger, more alert, and more alive than ever before. Sensory perception is enhanced considerably. I have found, for example, that all of my senses have become more acute with age, rather than less so, which is usually the case. This does not mean that if your vision is poor, as you start to practice the methods of power, your eyesight will correct itself. However, this actually has happened. Each of the senses is chakra related. As certain chakras are activated, there is corresponding heightening of particular senses. This experience is marvelous. Food has more flavor, colors are more luscious, you can appreciate subtle aromas, music has more dimension, and your sense of touch becomes very refined. The world becomes more of a playground of delights.

As Kundalini flow increases, your basic energy level usually improves. Sometimes people actually require more rest because they are undergoing great changes. But more often, energy is increased. You may find yourself more active, more stimulated. You may sleep less than before, and experience less variation in your energy level throughout the course of your day. When Kundalini is more active, you will find that you can easily will yourself to be more energetic if you do start to feel fatigued. This is a very helpful thing to be able to do for yourself.

Sleep changes too. As I mentioned before, you may find yourself sleeping less yet feeling better rested. There are a few other things that can occur. Dreams may become extraordinarily vivid, and in some cases prophetic. I have found that there is a correlation between activation of the chakras and various kinds of dreams. Dreams can become fantastic, violent, ethereal, profound, or lucid. In lucid dreaming, you are aware that you are dreaming, and may alter the course of the dream consciously while still asleep.

There are phenomena which are classic "Kundalini experiences." These can be ecstatic, scary, or just plain strange. I believe that the more prepared you are for them, the more enjoyable they are. The most common of these experiences is heat in the lower spine. Often the very base of the spine will heat up, as though you have been sitting in hot water. This can be quite a pleasurable experience. Sometimes this is accompanied by greatly increased sexual drives.

An experience which I had in my early days of practice was vibrating of the spine. Whenever I would sit in meditation, or perform breathing methods, my spine would quiver. This was not due to muscle fatigue or strain, but rather to an inner spinal impulse. It never happened at any time other than during practice, and it stopped after about a year.

One of the most exciting experiences is when a sudden burst of Kundalini energy rushes up the spine, through the chakra system. There is often a sensation of heat when this occurs, and sometimes a marvelous inner light show. Usually people experience a profound joy, a sense of great expansion, and waves of power pouring through them when Kundalini rushes up the spine. This is a time to focus your attention at the third eye, or to proceed with one of the meditation techniques described in the chapter on meditation. Another possibility is to relax, let go of all preconceived notions about what is to happen, and let the experience take you where it will.

It seems to be the case that most Kundalini experiences are short-lived. Usually they last for only several minutes, though you will feel the effects for days. Such an experience can leave you feeling clear minded, strong, and more enthusiastic about life.

Some Kundalini experiences can last appreciably longer. I know of people who have experienced heightened Kundalini activity for months at a time. I once experienced this for close to six weeks. I slept little, was very energetic, felt remarkably strong, and was in a constant ecstatic state. The purpose of all this information is to let you know what kinds of things are possible, and what may be in store for you if you work with methods of Kundalini development. At the same time, they are only experiences, which means that they are completely transitory. They are not everlasting, and they are not worth going after. Admittedly, such experiences are useful for inspirational purposes. In a sense, they are a confirmation that your practice is actually "doing something" for you. On the other hand, they are simply passing moments in time. Some people I know have never had any of these experiences, yet they are very high, very wise. So do not think that such events signify true spiritual growth. They signify that there is some specific energetic activity going on within you. But true spirituality is another matter altogether. That occurs when you integrate your power into a life which is conscious, growth-oriented, and exquisitely balanced.

9. Power Generators

In the development of power, there are many methods, many traditions. There are those who claim that if you want to develop your power fully, you must attach yourself to one teacher, one tradition, and one set of methods. In this manner, you will supposedly absorb the maximum value possible from the teachings you work with. I do not share this opinion. Nor do I recommend that you flutter from one method to another with a minimal span of attention. But there is value in synthesizing the best of many traditions, and approaching those methods seriously, thoughtfully, and with great discipline. With this in mind, I have attempted in this single work to draw from a variety of teachings and traditions, and assemble those methods which I believe to be most useful. It is entirely up to the reader to work with these methods, and to do so carefully and thoroughly.

I do not believe that there is any tradition or set of teachings which cannot be improved. Show me the tradition which is no longer being improved, and I will show you one which is sliding toward death. How did the great systems of yoga develop in the first place? People learned, refined, synthesized, and developed new methods. The yogas are still in transition. There is no end to what can be done with the body-mind. So we can keep on learning, adding, subtracting, mixing, and refining methods of power.

In my own travels, I have encountered and practiced the following three methods—The Solar Plexus Charging, Energy Polarization, and Chi Development techniques. They come from some lesser known yogic and martial traditions. Each method is unique and powerful, and well worth trying for a year or so. Even a few months of practice with each of these methods will enhance your practice.

The solar plexus chakra (Manipura) was described in the chapter on the Human Energy System. It is the center of Will, and is potentially enormously powerful. A well-developed solar plexus chakra is associated with tremendous energy, personal drive, and sheer persistence. This is the kind of strength needed to pursue the path of power with unflagging dedication. In other words, a well-developed solar plexus chakra is a handy thing to have.

The Tibetans develop this chakra via a series of meditations, all of which are part of the practice of Tum-Mo, the development of the inner fire. By this practice (as mentioned in chapter 1), they generate enough heat to remain in sub-zero Himalayan conditions, without clothing or any external source of heat.

Perhaps you do not need to hang out naked in the snow. Perhaps you do not have the time to dedicate yourself to the practice of Tum-Mo. But you may still wish to develop your solar plexus chakra to a great extent, and to promote the inner force in that center. It can be done with the Solar Plexus Charging Method. There are four aspects to this practice. They are posture, breath, color, and concentration. In previous methods, posture, breath and concentration have all been combined. Color is a new addition.

Colors are not just curious components of the visible-light spectrum. They are visible representations of specific vibrations and frequencies which have mental and psychic influences. To put it more simply, colors can affect the body-mind. Colors are used therapeutically for healing purposes. In fact, in Scandinavian and European countries, there are color-healing clinics. There is sufficient accumulated data to support the claim that color healing is a remarkable health-care system which has not received the attention it deserves.

That color affects the mind should come as no surprise. Almost everyone has had the experience of being repulsed by a particular-colored wall or room. Likewise, almost everyone has found certain colors soothing, pleasing, exciting. The psychic influences of color are no less dramatic. Colors affect energy flow, affect the opening of the chakras, and induce a variety of meditative states. A rich, golden color is stimulating to the solar plexus, which is why it is part of the Solar Plexus Charging Method. For further information on color, pick up a book on the subject. A good one is written by Ouseley.

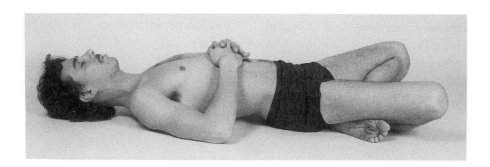

Solar Plexus Charging

Lie on your back in a dark, quiet place. Your head is facing north, your feet are facing south. Your legs are folded, as though you were sitting in a cross-legged position. Your hands are resting on your solar plexus, with the fingers interlocking.

Inhale slowly and steadily through the nose. As you do, picture a rich, golden light pouring in through your head, through your body, and into the abdomen, pelvis, and thighs.

As you exhale slowly and steadily (through either the nose or mouth), let the rich, golden light circle around the entire abdominal area in a clockwise direction. Your navel is the center of the clock. Twelve o'clock is at the sternum (the breast bone), and six o'clock is at the groin. As you exhale, let the energy circle clockwise, around and around. With every inhalation, bring the rich, golden light down into your abdominal area, and let that energy accumulate. With every exhalation, let that light and energy circle clockwise around your abdominal area, building heat as it goes. Practice this for a minimum of fifteen minutes.

As with many other methods, attention is everything. Keep your mind totally focused on the breath, the color, and the motion of the energy as you move it around the solar plexus.

You will build up heat if you practice this regularly. This method is short, simple, and remarkable. Do it for a year, and you may never get cold again.

Energy Polarization

Not all methods of power are as intense or dynamic as the Kundalini Yoga practices or Solar Plexus Charging. A case in point is the Energy Polarization technique. It truly empowers the body-mind. But it does so by relieving stress, reducing nervousness, and "washing" the entire human energy system with color and breath. The effect of this method is a more open, vital, tension-free body-mind. This too is power.

There are some people who mistake intensity for power, who mistake intensity for vitality. Intensity may be part of your growth. But stress can be intense, violence can be intense, anger can be intense. None of these is necessarily valuable for longevity, glowing health, and wisdom. In fact, too much intensity will burn you out. Excessive intensity can turn a person into a hollow shell. Vitality is a condition in which life-energy flows freely and unobstructed. It is a condition in which each cell of the body, each aspect of the body-mind, swims in this energy. You can be vital and relaxed. You can also be immensely powerful and relaxed. Observe a lion sometime. There is no more relaxed animal in the world than the lion at rest. But the lion on a hunt or in a fight is transformed into a living fury.

The Energy Polarization method empowers the body-mind by freeing it from all manner of tensions, so that it can be increasingly vital. If you suffer from nervousness, stress, insomnia, or tension, this method is absolutely for you. As with the Solar Plexus Charging technique, this method utilizes posture, breath, color, and concentration.

Lie down on your back on a firm surface. Your spine should be warm, so lie on a carpet or blanket or animal skin. Your head is pointed north, and your feet are pointing south. Your hands are touching your sides with the palms turned upward. Your eyes are closed. Inhale slowly and steadily through the nose. As you do, draw a warm, golden light in through the top of your head, down through your entire body, and out your feet. Then, as you exhale (through either the mouth or nose), draw a cool, soothing, blue light in through the soles of your feet, up through your body, and out the top of your head. Repeat this over and over, with a steady, even breath. With each breath, feel energy circulating down through you and then up through you. Practice this for a minimum of fifteen minutes.

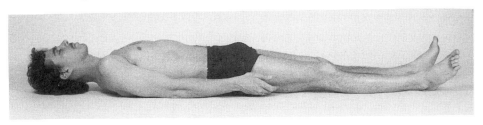

There are three aspects to the "polarization" in this method. The first has to do with the cardinal directions, north and south. By aligning your body with these, you lock into the polarity of the earth. This helps to align your energy system with the energy flow of the earth itself. Secondly there is color. The golden color is stimulating and enlivening, and the blue is cooling and soothing. The alternation of these colors throughout your body-mind activates vitality and relaxation at the same time. Finally, there is the connection between the colors you are using and the sun and moon. The golden color is related to the sun, energetically speaking. The cool blue is related to the moon.

With the Energy Polarization method, you are dealing with Yin and Yang, sun and moon, day and night, activity and rest. The body-mind itself is a blend of all manner of polarities. By performing the Energy Polarization method, you enable yourself to experience a broad range of healthful conditions, easily and naturally.

Chi Development Method

To be sure, there are as many methods of power as there are people to practice. Among the Chinese systems of Kung Fu, Tai Chi, and Chi Kung, countless methods abound. In one way or another, each of these methods is used to stimulate the flow of Chi, the intrinsic force which resides in the *Hara*, the spot below the navel. The development of Chi usually requires extensive training, but there are some techniques which work quickly and easily. While extensive and rigorous training will produce results that are not obtained by a more abbreviated practice, not everyone has hours of time to develop Chi. With this in mind, I present the following technique. It is very simple, takes fifteen minutes daily, and will make you feel lighter, more clear-minded, stronger, and more energetic.

Chi is not some vague phenomenon. It is a power which can be used and demonstrated. I have had great Chi demonstrated on me, and it is a strange thing indeed. Several years ago I had a radio show on a small station near Boston. On my show I interviewed unusual guests, and one week I had a guest who had mastered Chi to a great extent (so he said). He was quite small—short in height and very slim. I was bigger than him by far, and much better muscled. After the show, I told him that I was curious to see some sort of demonstration of his Chi, just to satisfy my own curiosity. The master consented, and recommended that I assume a stable standing position. I did. He moved his arm near my abdomen, muscles relaxed and wrist loose and limp. With a light, gentle motion, he tapped my abdomen. What I saw and what I felt were two different things!

What I saw was a very light tap on the belly. What I felt was something like a refrigerator pushing my entire torso, just one time, very hard, until I hit the wall that had been about six feet behind me. "Wait a minute," I said. "Let's try that one more time." This time I really dug in, assumed a lower, better-grounded stance. Once more the master tapped me very lightly on the belly. There was no tension in his arm, no muscular push. Again I flew. That was a demonstration of Chi. People can do remarkable things with it.

If you practice a martial art, the following method will be of value to you in your practice. If you simply wish to improve your overall vitality, this practice is a convenient way to achieve that outcome.

Sit in a comfortable cross-legged position. Take several long, slow, deep breaths. Inhale through the nose, and exhale through the mouth. The tip of your tongue touches the upper palate at all times. With your left hand, cover your right ear lightly but completely. Breathe long and slow, and relax more with each breath. Do this for five minutes. Then switch so that your right hand covers your left ear in the same manner, and continue breathing for another five minutes. With each breath, relax even more. For the last five minutes, cover both ears with the opposite hands, with your right arm over your left. Breathe and relax, breathe and relax.

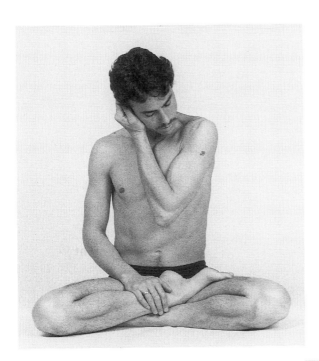

This is one of a very few methods in which you slump, relax, and do not maintain a straight spine. You must relax with each breath, reducing tension as you go.

10. Siva's High Magic —
The Invocation of the Shadow

In the entire history of the Yogic and Hindu traditions of the East, no figure stands as majestically or shines as brightly as Siva, King of the Yogis. Encoiled by serpents, he is the Destroyer, the shatterer of illusion, the explosive force of pure God realization, working through the hearts and minds of his devotees, and upon the entire world as well. He is described as *Mahadeva*, the Great God, above all other gods, worshiped even by Krishna. His forms are countless, as the following description indicates:

"He assumes many forms of gods (as Brahma, Visnu, Indra, Rudra) and of men, of goblins, demons, barbarians, tame and wild beasts, birds, reptiles, fishes, with many varieties of human disguises, etc. He is the soul of all the worlds, all-pervading, residing in the heart of all creatures, knowing all desires. He carries a discus, a trident, a club, a sword, and an axe. He has a girdle of serpents, ear-rings of serpents, a sacrificial cord of serpents, an outer garment of serpents' skins. He laughs, sings, dances charmingly, and plays various musical instruments. He leaps, gapes, weeps, makes others weep; speaks like a madman or a drunkard, as well as in sweet tones. He laughs terrifically. He is both visible and invisible, on the altar, on the sacrificial post, in the fire, a boy, an old man, a youth. He dallies with the daughters and the wives of the Rishis with erect hair, obscene appearance, naked, with excited look. He is one-faced, two-faced, three-faced, many-faced."

Siva is a mixture of all possible attributes. He is sweet, loving, terrifying, a fiery rage, the master Yogi, the invincible warrior. His third eye contains all revelations, and through it all the mysteries of the Universe can be known. He can reduce mountains to dust, and liberate the lowest of the low. In all of creation, none of the gods, Siddhas, sages, Yogis or adepts can match his awesome power. Siva is the one, eternal reigning king, the Master of all masters.

The discourses of Siva, usually given to his consort Parvati, are extensive expositions of Yogic techniques. The *Yoganusasanam* (the Great Yogic Sermon), the *Vigyana Bhairava Tantra* (an elaborate description of 108 Yogic methods), and the *Siva Samhita* are just a few of the many volumes of Siva's discourses. These discourses bear testimony to the limitless knowledge of Lord Siva, and to the endless variety of forms with which he works. There are descriptions of yogic postures, breathing techniques, use of mantras, meditations for the arousal of Kundalini, and a vast treasure trove of techniques and methods for all people and situations.

Perhaps the strangest practice of all, however, is found in the *Siva Samhita*. The Invocation Of The Shadow is a high magic technique involving the building of a form which is then imbued with power, which then empowers the practitioner. This practice is simple, easy, and can be practiced by anyone with moderately good eyesight.

According to Siva, the Invocation of the Shadow enables one to see the unseen, to behold God, to increase life span, avoid accidental death, become fully happy, destroy sin, increase virtue, and eventually attain liberation from the cycle of death and rebirth. He states that the Yogi who engages in the Invocation of the Shadow becomes victorious, and can go anywhere. These are indeed remarkable claims from the king of the Yogis.

The actual technique of the Invocation of the Shadow (*pratikopasana*) is as follows:

Either in sunlight or by moonlight, fix your attention on the neck of your own shadow. After focusing on this for a moment, look up into the sky. If you see a full grey shadow in the sky, then that is auspicious, and you have successfully engaged in the practice. You may do this several times in a row, though Siva says that whenever the shadow is seen for even a single second in the sky, you behold God in the sky at that very moment.

Siva recommends that the Invocation of the Shadow be practiced daily, and says that it is of particular value during times of trouble, or upon commencing travel, auspicious work, or marriage. Furthermore, he states that by practicing this invocation always, one sees the shadow in one's own heart, and is liberated.

It is the plight of the unenlightened that we often fail to perceive the miraculous, even though miracles and Godlight are always around us. So too, the Invocation of the Shadow appears to be little more than an optical trick—a matter of focusing on a dark object and then seeing it reversed lighter against the sky. It can be explained away as simply as that, if one approaches it from the viewpoint of basic science. Approached from the viewpoint of high magic, however, the Invocation of the Shadow demands careful consideration.

Siva's entire exposition of the Siva Samhita is predicated upon the presumption of our own Godliness. It is never an issue that must be first addressed, clarified, or proven. Our absolute divinity is a foregone conclusion, and is the starting point for all other considerations. This attitude lies at the very heart of the Invocation of the Shadow, and it is understood that this practice is simply a means for identifying more strongly with our own Godliness. Thus one enters into the invocation with this understanding, one which is essential for any further progress and realization.

With the presumption of one's own divinity as a working base, the next step is to become engaged with the powerful, elemental forces of the sun or moon. Representing the masculine and feminine forces of our world respectively, the sun and moon exert themselves upon us, either by direct light or by reflection, causing us to throw a shadow. Gazing upon the shadow, we are observing the product which results from the interaction of the sun or moon and our own body-mind. The shadow is an effect which takes place as we mingle with potent solar or lunar forces. In the yogic scriptures it is stated many times that the entire manifest Universe is made of energy and light. As we observe the shadow, we witness what happens when different forces of energy and light react with one another.

After focusing on the shadow, the next step is to gaze into the sky, where the shadow becomes visible as a luminous form. This change in perspective turns the shadow into a celestial body, huge and glowing in the sky. The sighting of this is an experience in the relative nature of all things. Once the shadow was just a dark patch that followed us everywhere. But for a moment it is transformed into a divine sight. It is just like the Self, through which divine light is pouring all the time. But the personality, like a physical body, stands between the divine light of the Self and its projection upon the world. We usually manifest only a shadowy reflection of the Self, the divine being within us. But an alteration of perspective can enable one to see and manifest divinity more strongly, with great purity. This is the process of enlightenment. When we observe the shadow in the sky, an opportunity is created for a shift in perspective that is more than just optical. The effect is a greater sense of being God, and a cleansing of aspects of personality which are obstructions to God-realization.

This magical process of seeing can alter everything for a person. As with any other technique, ritual, or observance, the Invocation of the Shadow must be performed with a fresh attitude and an open mind every day. Otherwise it can become a meaningless and perfunctory performance of the limitations of non-awareness. But practiced with a keen and open mind, the Invocation of the Shadow can be a catalyst for tremendous change. Who is projecting what? Is the body merely throwing a shadow because it is obstructing a non-intelligent light? The presumption of divinity allows us to know that everything is divine, and that all of what we see, feel, and know is a part of the play of God.

By regular practice of the Invocation of the Shadow, the power of realization is absorbed into the spiritual heart. One's presumption of Godliness becomes a thorough realization, a condition of being which is no longer reliant upon intellectual consideration. As this realization eradicates all other possibilities for a person, then there is liberation from the cycle of time and karma, just as Siva has stated.

We live in a completely magical world which is made mundane only by our inability to perceive life for what it is—a marvelous expression of divine play. The Invocation of the Shadow is a means by which one's perspective can be altered, allowing for the rediscovery of our own true nature.

11. Cosmic Meditation

Language is an odd thing. It is a complex scheme of symbols which are used to describe, or represent, things, activities, people, places, ideas, and so on. The word "dog," for example, is not the animal itself, but a representation of the beast. The word conjures an idea, or image, in one's mind of a particular kind of creature. When I hear the word "dog," for example, I am likely to think of a golden retriever. Another person may think of a bloodhound. Yet we all basically understand the word "dog."

Language is very useful, in that it allows for some kind of understanding between people. However, it is essential to understand that language is purely symbolic. I may verbally describe an experience to you, and you may verbally acknowledge that description with an affirmative reply, or a description of something which seems to be a similar experience of your own. In actuality, I cannot verbally convey any experience at all. The only way to understand an experience is to live it oneself.

You may wonder why I am spending so much time describing the limitations of language. The reason is that this is a chapter on meditation. Meditation is lived and experienced. It is breathed and felt. It is a current which moves through your soul. As you read this section, you must know that whatever is written here is only the barest approximation, merely a collection of symbols, which describe something vast, potent, and magical. Just as the word "orgasm" in no way even hints of that experience, so do all descriptions of meditation fall laughably short of saying much about meditation itself. With the word "dog," there is at least some common point of reference to lend sensibility to a discussion of the animal. For meditation, the sensibility of discussion is tenuous at best. Nonetheless, if what is written here can spark even a vague sense of what meditation is about, then language has not failed us after all. Consider all descriptions that follow as teases— hinting of more, flirting with your understanding. There is much, much more than what there seems to be.

Not only is meditation hard to describe, but there is widespread disagreement about what meditation is. Some say meditation is a technique; some say it is a state of being; some say it is simply being. Each is correct. There are in fact many methods, or techniques, of meditation. From *zazen*, to mantra meditation, to listening to the sounds within one's own head, there are actually thousands of methods, or ways, to meditate. When you engage in any one of these practices, you may find yourself in a "meditative state," in which your mind is clear and alert, yet without thought or clutter. There are people for whom meditation is their being. That is, they need not sit and contemplate anything in particular. Rather, they are "in meditation" always, whether sitting quietly, walking, eating, making love, or moving their bowels. Consider the possibility that meditation is a fundamental condition of existence. Another way to say this is that meditation, or total, spontaneous awareness, is the natural human condition.

Meditation methods lead to meditative states, which lead to being meditation. This chapter deals with the practice of meditation, or Cosmic Meditation. Cosmic? Everything in the Universe is one. "Uni" means One. So we are all actually one with everything else. In fact, there really is no such thing as "else," but we think there is. It is exactly because we live with a dualistic attitude—the notion of I and Other—that we need to meditate in the first place. So to say "Cosmic" Meditation is to remind the reader that meditation is for being at One. Like I said before, words do not really hack it when it comes to meditation.

In any case, this chapter is about meditation practice, and about some things which may occur during that practice. In keeping with the rest of the material in this book, the meditation practices described here are very powerful. They trigger a variety of profound experiences, and are effective for directing power through the entire body-mind. I have worked with each one for at least several years. While my personal experience does not authenticate any method, my teaching experience with these methods certainly does. Hundreds of people I know have achieved marvelous results with these methods. Each technique is old, taken from traditional yoga practices of the Hindus.

Before describing any of the methods, one question begs an answer. Why meditate? What is the purpose of such an endeavor? To answer, let's consider the Four Noble Truths of Buddha. Buddha taught that: (1) life is suffering, that (2) the cause of all suffering is ignorance, that (3) there is an end to suffering, and that (4) the end to suffering is the Way, or the Path.

Buddha's Four Noble Truths are based on the understanding that each person lives in a dualistic state. We perceive the world in terms of "I" and "Other." We are therefore totally unaware of our true nature, which is Being at One with every-thing. **I AM THAT I AM,** is the best way to say it. Our dualistic mentality breeds antagonism, lust, anger, greed, fear, attachment, and all manner of "suffering." But, he says, there is an end to all this pain, and that is the Way, or the Path. The Path is the spiritual journey. Meditation is an integral part of this journey. It **IS** the journey. Meditation is the key joint of the archway to freedom. It is the means by which One-ness is comprehended and lived.

Not everyone would describe life as suffering. The word "suffering" is so severe. However, everyone has suffered at one time or another, so we can appreciate what that is about. By definition, a cluttered mind is suffering. Confusion, unhappiness, misunderstanding, are all suffering. So what are we to do, become homogenized, unfeeling beings? Not at all. Meditation promises an alteration of the way we perceive living. All phenomena are understood as "play," as footsteps and move-ments in a great, strange, intricate dance. That dance is the dance of *Maya*, or Illusion.

One undertakes the practice of meditation to clear the mind, to sweep accumu-lated debris from one's attention, and to perceive each moment in as fresh, clear, and joyful a manner as possible. I do not know anyone who can not use a little bit of that. This world is overwhelming and strange, like a wild storm. Anything which can help us to ride the crest of the gale is worth knowing.

If you meditate, you will almost certainly have some unusual experiences. Much as with the practice of Kundalini Yoga, strange and interesting phenomena may occur inside you. Sensations, sights, and sounds of all kinds are common. These experiences can be very exciting—and fun. Enjoy them, and let them go. Meditation should be approached with a completely fresh attitude, and without expectations. Why? Because the greatest benefits of meditation lie far beyond what we comprehend, or expect. If you meditate expecting something in particular, you may prevent the occurrence of something even greater.

Approach meditation with great care. Set aside time to meditate without interruption. Make sure that you are clean and comfortable. Afford yourself a special place (a corner of a room—almost anywhere will do) which is reserved only for meditation. Keep that place neat, clean, and attractive. Set a mood for yourself by honoring where you practice. Keep flowers there if you can. Meditate for the love of it. As with other methods, avoid practicing on a full stomach. The early morning and evening are wonderful times to meditate. Your practice is the most uniquely liberating opportunity you will ever have.

Kundalini Yoga Meditation

Just as all systems of yoga activate the Kundalini energy to some extent, so do all forms of meditation stir this latent force within us. However, some methods arouse the Kundalini more directly, quickly, and powerfully than others. This Kundalini Meditation is a case in point. It is a fairly simple and straightforward method. It is not particularly difficult, and it does not require an enormous time investment. It is performed comfortably in about thirty-five or forty-five minutes. The reward is that the results are steady and powerful.

Maybe the word "results" is a little funny to use in a description about meditation. After all, so much of what happens in the meditation process is not quantifiable. However, blockages in the human energy system are removed fairly easily by this method. The mind clears easily, and you will feel a great deal stronger than prior to practice. Those are the kinds of results that can be observed and enjoyed by anyone who will devote the time and attention required to practice this method daily.

Let's begin. Seat yourself comfortably in a cross-legged position. Full lotus is ideal, but this may not be practical for you. Any other easy cross-legged position is fine, provided you keep your spine straight. Your hands are on your knees. Your eyes are closed, your mouth is closed, and the tip of your tongue is touching your upper palate.

In this position, breathe steadily and easily through the nose for several minutes. As you do this, relax any unnecessary tension in your muscles, and let your mind clear.

Then direct your attention to the first chakra, Muladhara, at the perineum, the spot at the very base of the spine, between the anus and the genitals. Focus your attention there for about three minutes or so, breathing slowly and fully. With each breath, feel as though you are breathing right through that center of energy.

From there, move your attention to the second chakra, Svadhisthana, located along the lower spine, at the area of the genitals. Focus your attention there for about three minutes or so, breathing slowly and fully. As you breathe, let the energy of the breath flow through the second chakra.

The next point of attention is the third chakra, Manipura, located along the spine at the area of the solar plexus. Focus your attention there for about three minutes or so, breathing slowly and fully. Let the energy of the breath flow through the solar plexus area.

From there, move your awareness to the fourth chakra, Anahata, located along the spine at the very center of the chest. Focus your attention there for about three minutes, breathing slowly and fully. As you breathe, send the energy of the breath right through the center of the chest.

Next, focus on the fifth chakra, Visudha, located in the center of your throat. Focus your attention there for about three minutes, breathing slowly and fully. As you breathe, let the energy of the breath pass through the entire throat area.

From the throat, raise your attention to the sixth chakra, Ajna, the third eye. This is located at the root of the nose, between and slightly above the eyebrows. Focus at this point for about three minutes, breathing slowly and fully. As you breathe, send the energy in and out of the third eye.

Next, bring your attention to the seventh chakra, Sahasrara, the crown of the head. Focus at this point for about three minutes, breathing slowly and fully. As you breathe, let the energy of the breath radiate from the crown.

From the crown, bring your attention to the spot about eight inches above the crown. As though there were a halo of light there, concentrate at this point for about three minutes, breathing slowly and fully. As you breathe, concentrate the energy of the breath at this spot.

From there, send your attention up, up, into the heavens, and visualize the moon and sun above you, to the left and right respectively. Focus on these celestial bodies for about three minutes or so, breathing slowly and fully.

Once this is done, bring your attention back to your third eye. Relax at this center, keeping your attention focused, with the breath steady and full. Keep your attention here for ten minutes, or as much longer as you wish.

When you are done, take one or two long, deep breaths, exhaling through the mouth. Then rub your hands together vigorously, and rub them all over your face. Slowly open your eyes, and relax for a minute or two before becoming more active.

What this meditation does is open up the chakra system, and infuse it with a tremendous amount of prana—the energy of the breath. The breath is key to this meditation, as is attention. At each energy center, keep your attention as focused as possible. Keep the breath steady and full. This will fuel your meditation, and provide the necessary conditions to activate the Kundalini energy. If you practice this meditation, do so for at least a year or two. Longer is desirable.

Nad Yoga: Sound Current Meditation

In the active practice of meditation, there are many phenomena which you will encounter. One of these is the *Nada*, or sound current. The Nada is a vibrational current, a ripple of sound, if you will, which courses through absolutely everything. As you know, atoms and their components are busily zipping around at a great rate. Does it surprise you to consider that these fast-moving particles might make a bit of noise? Actually, it is not the atoms themselves which make noise (to my knowledge), but the energy which underlies them which produces the sound current.

If you meditate regularly, the sound current is a phenomenon which you can expect to encounter. When you will encounter it is most likely during meditation. Why you will encounter it is that meditation practice enlivens your senses, including your hearing. For you encounter the Nada by hearing it. The sound current is actually hundreds, maybe thousands of sounds. Initially you may hear it as one, simple tone. But in time it can become orchestral.

The sound current is initially best heard in a sound-free or relatively quiet environment. If you practice the Kundalini Yoga Meditation in a quiet place, for example, you may hear a slight buzzing or ringing in the ears, especially the right ear. This is not the sound of blood rushing through the ears; blood does not make a high-pitched whine or buzz as it flows. Nor should the sound be confused with *Meniere's Disease*, a condition which creates a loud ringing in the ears and loss of balance. What you hear is the sound current. This simple, seemingly innocuous tone is actually a gateway to fantastic worlds.

It seems to me that the easiest way to discuss the Nada, the sound current, is to describe the Nad Yoga, the actual meditation upon this sound. I recommend two ways to practice. One is to perform the Nad Yoga by itself, and the second is to do the Kundalini Yoga Meditation prior to practice of the meditation on the sound current. At the end of the Kundalini Yoga Meditation, you can either continue to sit up, or lie down. The second way is simply to enhance the practice of the method which follows. The advantage to preceeding Nad Yoga with the Kundalini Yoga Meditation is that you will generate a lot of energy with the Kundalini method. This almost always intensifies the Nad Yoga Meditation. However, this method is also time-consuming. I recommend that you try both ways and then practice the one which seems to suit you best.

Nad Yoga, or Sound Current Meditation, attunes you to the resonance of highly refined sounds which course through creation. The practice of this simple meditation makes tremendous mind expansion possible, and opens up a multidimensional awareness in those who practice it.

This method is best practiced lying down. Yet it is necessary to be alert enough to stay awake, rather than drifting off to sleep. Unlike some meditation practices which are popular these days, falling asleep during practice is not useful during Sound Current Meditation. This method can be performed sitting up, but the initial effects are not as profound as when lying down. Lie on a firm, flat surface with no pillow. Keep your legs straight and uncrossed, and your arms by your sides with the palms of your hands turned upward. Relax as much as you can, loosening muscular and mental tension. It is important to be in a quiet, dark place. It is ideal to practice at night or in the early morning when the rest of the world is still. If noise is a problem, earplugs can be used.

With your eyes and mouth closed (this is important), turn all your attention to the inside of your head, and begin to listen carefully. Concentrate on the right side of the head, near the inner ear. There will be a sound of some sort. You may hear a light ringing sound, a soft buzzing sound, or something akin to a faint rumble. Listen as closely as possible to whatever sound you hear, with absolute attention. Listen as though you are trying to hear someone who is in another room speaking in a whisper.

As you listen, the sound you hear will grow louder, and you will start to hear other sounds. In fact, so many sounds may start to swell at once that the original sound may be lost. As the sounds become louder, focus your attention on just one, as though you were trying to pay attention to just one instrument in a symphony. Concentrate intently on that one sound. It will become louder and louder, and you may in time experience the sensation of that sound resonating through your entire body-mind. As you listen carefully, the sound may turn into something else, something subtler, more refined. Go with that, and keep your attention as focused as possible.

There are many sounds you may hear: bells, flutes, falling water, the sound of the ocean, the singing of birds, and more. As you practice this meditation regularly, you will hear ever subtler sounds, rarer tones. However, you must pay very close attention, or all the sounds will fade away.

When you meditate on the sound current, you attune your attention to the source of the sound. With practice, you experience becoming one with the sound. By this experience, you become familiar with a wide range of altered states, and heightened awareness. Begin practicing Nad Yoga for at least fifteen minutes, increasing the time to as long as you want.

The experience of the Nada is like no other. You cannot imagine what it is like to play with the sound current until you do it. The sounds you hear are like no others. To find yourself bathed in the rare vibrations of the sound current is exquisite. The trick to success with this practice is persistence. You will find that sounds are very slippery. They come and go, they disappear, they change. Listen, listen, listen. Focus your attention. By doing this, you will enjoy some fantastic experiences, and develop increasingly keen perceptual abilities.

Silver Cord Meditation

In the *Vigyana Bhairava Tantra*, one of the discourses of Siva, there is reference to a meditation upon a fine cord which runs through the spine. The cord is actually sushumna, the central channel of the human energy system. The meditation is very powerful.

I recommend that the Silver Cord Meditation be preceded by the Kundalini Yoga Meditation. My reason for this recommendation is that the Kundalini meditation generates a lot of energy, and also enhances powers of concentration and visualization, which are essential to the Silver Cord Meditation. I think that the Kundalini Yoga Meditation can be performed prior to any other method, and will only enhance the particular technique you practice. With that in mind, let us proceed to the Silver Cord Meditation.

Sit in a cross-legged position—lotus is preferred—with your spine very straight, and your eyes closed. Your hands are resting on your knees. Direct your full attention to your spine. Visualize the full length of it, and all the vertebrae. If you are not sure what your spine looks like, consult an anatomical chart. Picture that in the very center of your spine there is a long, fine silver cord which runs the entire length of the spine, from the very base to the top of your skull. The core of the silver cord is a brilliant crimson red.

With every breath, focus your attention on the silver cord with the red core. Visualize it in its entirety. This is absolutely all there is to the actual method of the Silver Cord Meditation. Simply focus on the cord, and picture it in your mind.

At first this meditation may seem overly simple. But it is a method which requires resolute attention, and tremendous concentration. As you hold the image of the silver cord in your mind, the Kundalini energy streams through the cord, energizing the entire chakra system. You start to expand, slowly at first, and then much more rapidly. It is not uncommon to feel as though you are floating in space, like one tiny atom suspended in an ocean of energy. This meditation will not only expand your awareness and provide you with some fabulous meditative states, but it is also effective for dissolving blockages in the chakra system, and increasing overall energy.

As with any other meditation, I recommend that you practice this one regularly and consistently, for at least a year or so. That seems to be the only way to determine the value of a method of this kind. Coupled with the Kundalini Yoga Meditation, this is a very substantial meditation practice. Do this for as long as you like.

Center of the Skull

Over a decade ago, I found a reference to a little known meditation in an obscure yogic text. With no direct personal instruction, I began practice of what I refer to here as the Center of the Skull Meditation. What started out as an inquiry based primarily on curiosity, turned into the most rewarding meditation practice I have been priviledged to experience. The Center of the Skull Meditation is what I would refer to as a "key joint." In a structure there is often a key joint, a point where, when pressure is applied, the entire structure is affected. This meditation is such a key joint. When attention is directed toward this practice, the entire structure of your consciousness is affected. How you are aware, how much you are aware, and of what you are aware, will be altered in a positive, often spectacular manner by this practice.

To benefit fully from this method, consider the Kundalini Yoga Meditation to be a prerequisite. Begin this method with the Kundalini practice, and then continue without a break. The Kundalini Yoga Meditation activates the chakras, and that is essential to the Center of the Skull practice. The reason this is so important is that, with this practice, the object is to draw the Kundalini to the center of the skull. While this can be accomplished without first practicing the Kundalini method, progress is slower.

The Center of the Skull Method is very simple. After completing the Kundalini method, bring your attention to the very center of the skull. How do you know where that is? If you ran a straight line from the top of one ear to the top of the other, and intersected it with a line which ran from the very center of the top of your head straight down, that point of intersection is where you want to focus your attention. Or, there is another way to find it. Breathe slowly and steadily through your nose. As you inhale, the breath runs up your nostrils, and above your upper palate. In your mind, run a short line straight up from the center of your upper palate, up through where the breath passes, and about half-an-inch further up. Right there is where you focus your attention.

With your attention at that spot, your mouth closed, and the tip of your tongue against your upper palate, breathe slowly, steadily, and somewhat deeply through your nose. Take long, slow inhalations, and long, slow exhalations. Let the breath pass by the spot at the center of the skull, in and out, over and over. This is all you have to do. Breathe steadily, without a break, and keep your unwavering attention at the center of the skull. As a thought bubbles up into your conscious-ness, just let it go. Breathe, and let it go. As thoughts come up again and again, just breathe and let them go. Keep your attention only at the center of the skull.

Since it would be a shame to try (ineffectively) to describe what can happen during this practice, I will refrain. Suffice it to say that I have never encountered any method as substantial, powerful, and radical as this one. Practice it regularly, and practice it carefully. I would practice this for no more than forty-five minutes or so for the first year. After that you can really extend the time as long as you like. If you can practice this both morning and night, it will change your waking and sleeping hours, energize you, and make your dreams very interesting.

I have found that this method promotes spontaneous out-of-body experiences. The way to make this occur is to practice the meditation, and then when you are through, lie down on your back in Corpse Pose. In this position, you lie flat on your back, eyes closed, feet about ten inches apart, arms about ten inches from your sides, with your palms up. As you breathe, let all of your muscles relax, as though they would fall away from your bones. When you are fully relaxed, let yourself drift with your breath. In this position, you may suddenly bolt (or drift) out of your body. The experience is unlike any other, because with all other ex-periences you are still in the body.

In an out-of-body experience, the body-mind is actually intact, but the body that you travel in is astral, much finer than the physical one that you walk around in all day. Its time/space/distance limitations are few, and it can travel very, very quickly. There are many books on out-of-body travel, and I do not intend to write one here. Such travel opens up new worlds, which if you are brave and curious, you will find utterly fantastic, and pleasurable beyond your wildest dreams.

So, that is a little bit about the Center of the Skull meditation. If you are inclined to undergo a radical transformation of consciousness, practice this method daily for several years. May your travels be wonderful.

Glossary

Acupuncture—An Oriental science of healing in which needles are inserted into "points" on the body through which energy flows. Acupuncture is based upon the Wu-Hsing, or Five Element Theory, in which all influences within or outside of the human body result from the interaction of the Five Elements, which compose the entire phenomenal world.

Ajna—The Third Eye. The chakra, or energy vortex, located between the eyes, at the root of the nose. Also known as the Mystic Eye, or All-Seeing Eye. The center of clairvoyance, supranormal vision.

Anahata—The Heart Chakra, or energy vortex, located along the spine at the center of the chest. The center of love and compassion.

Aura—The field of energy which emanates from, and surrounds, every person. Visible to some individuals, the aura is an indicator of health, vitality, energy level, and state of mind.

Buddha Hands Kung Fu—A combat system which originated from Tibet around 3,000 years ago. A particularly powerful martial art, specifically designed for mortal combat, armed or unarmed.

Cerebrospinal Fluid (CSF)—A viscous, yellow fluid which flows through the spinal column and the brain. Yogis of various traditions believe that specific Yogic practices change the CSF, making it a potent, mind-altering elixir.

Chakras—Vortices of energy within a person, located along the spine. Chakra locations correspond to the locations of various organs, glands, and nerve plexuses. The chakras are associated with particular aspects of human personality, and states of mind.

Chi—Life energy. Also known as Ki, Kundalini, The Force. In classical Chinese yogic philosophy (Taoism), Chi is the one unifying force of all creation.

Chi Kung—A group of various practices involving posture, breath, and motion, to arouse and circulate Chi throughout the entire body mind system. Chi Kung is currently being studied by the medical world for its unusual anaesthetic potential.

Chuang Fu—A group of Tibetan Yoga exercises practiced as a warm-up routine prior to practice of Buddha Hands Kung Fu.

Clairvoyance—Literally "clear seeing." The ability to see the past, present, and future. Clairvoyants can often see auras and other energy emanations.

Color Healing—A system of healing which utilizes colored lights, colored liquids, and color visualization techniques, to treat virtually every known ailment. Color healing has

120

found broad acceptance in Europe and Scandinavia, where one can find color healing clinics.

Cosmic Consciousness—A state of absolute awareness of, and unity with, the primary, creative intelligence of the Universe.

Dragon—In ancient Oriental mythology, an immortal winged serpent, lord of the under-world, and ruler of the skies.

Drugs (mind altering)—Traditionally, substances of botanical origin which are used to alter one's state of consciousness. There are in excess of 150 well-documented botanical drugs which have been used for ritual and non-ritual mind-altering purposes, many for thousands of years. Today there are also potent synthetic analogues of naturally-occurrng botanical drugs, as well as new classes of synthetically produced mind-altering substances.

Ecstasy—Unbridled joy, exhilaration, and fulfillment.

Five Elements—Wood, fire, earth, metal, and water. The theory of the Five Elements, or Wu Hsing, is a traditional Oriental model for understanding the phenomenal world. The Five Elements represent permutations of Chi, the one unifying force of creation.

Five Elements Exercises—A set of exercises involving posture, motion, breath, and con-centration. These exercises are designed to balance the flow of the Five Elements, which represent various temperaments and humors, through the body-mind system.

Five Tibetans—A group of five unusual exercises originating from Tibet, designed to balance the energy of the chakras, or energy vortices, of the body-mind system. This set of exercises is also reputed to promote dynamic health and longevity.

Hara—A spot located below the navel, regarded by various Oriental traditions i.e. Zen Buddhism, to be the center of power (Ki, Chi) within a person. A strong, well-developed Hara is a sign of great mastery.

Hatha Yoga—The traditional Hindu system of Yoga practice, which includes posture, breathing, concentration, methods of purification, austerities, devotion, and adherence to dietary and behavioral guidelines.

Karma Yoga—Work performed selflessly, often in devotion to a particular deity, or to some sort of spiritual ideal. Karma Yoga is a term commonly given to work in monastic and spiritual communities.

Ki—see Chi.

Kundalini—also known as Kundalini Shakti. The primary life force, the primary evolu-tionary force, and the seat of genius in all human beings. Described in the Yogic scrip-tures as a serpent or a goddess, Kundalini is the energy of the body-mind system.

Kundalini Experiences—Phenomena associated with the increased flow of Kundalini energy through the body-mind. These can include extremely heightened sensory aware-ness, acute stimulation of the body, out-of-body experiences, jolts of energy up the spine, and a vast array of non-typical occurrences. These experiences are typically associated with certain stages of Yoga practice.

Kung Fu—A generic term for any of a variety of Oriental martial arts.

Lotus Pose—The primary sitting posture of most Yoga traditions, and of virtually all Asian schools of meditation. Lotus pose involves crossing the legs, one over another, and maintaining an erect spinal posture. Lotus pose encourages the increased flow of Kundalini energy.

Manipura—The solar plexus chakra, or vortex of energy. Located along the spine near the solar plexus, this center is associated with personal power, charisma, and will.

Maya—Illusion. In Hindu and Buddhist traditions, Maya is the illusory play of life, and distracts us from comprehending the essence of existence.

Meridians—Energy channels. Lines of force which run throughout the body, through which Chi flows. The meridians are used in acupuncture, for the proper placement of needles. The meridians are also considered in Chi Kung, and in a variety of Oriental martial arts, including Tai Chi.

Microcosmic Orbit—A circle of energy which runs from the perineum (the spot between the anus and the genitals), up the spine, over the head to the upper lip, and from the lower lip down the front of the body, to the perineum. In the Taoist scheme (traditional Chinese Nature-based philosophy), the Microcosmic Orbit represents the Cosmos in man. Meditation upon this orbit is said to awaken one to cosmic consciousness.

Muladhara—The root chakra, or energy vortex. Located near the perineum, at the base of the spine. Associated with the consciousness of basic survival.

Nada—A current of sound which courses through everything. The Nada, or sound current, is audible, primarily in the right ear. Meditation upon the sound current is one of the most powerful Yoga practices available.

Out-of-Body Experience (oobe)—An occurrence in which the consciousness of a person leaves the physical body, without death as a result. During an out-of-body experience, people often observe their own physical body. One can see and hear during such an experience. Out-of-body travel is common among those whose step out of the body. During an out-of-body experience, one resides in a refined, energy body.

Perineum—The spot between the anus and the genitals. Where the Kundalini energy resides. Also the location of Muladhara, the root chakra.

Power—The capacity to act, or influence. Power is needed to perform any activity at all.

Prana—Energy taken into the body via the breath.

Pranayam—Controlled breathing. Specific breathing practices, designed to regulate the flow of energy in and out of the body-mind system.

Sahasrara—The crown chakra, or energy vortex. The center of energy at the top of the head. Associated with Cosmic Consciousness.

Shakti—Another term for power, Kundalini, Chi. Also refers to the female aspect of divine power.

Siddha—An accomplished Yogi who has developed supranormal or occult powers. A siddha may demonstrate unusual powers of self-control, such as the ability to maintain a perfectly healthy body temperature in sub-zero conditions, without clothing. Other powers include clairvoyance, levitation, materialization.

Svadhisthana—The sex chakra, or energy vortex. Located along the spine near the genitals. Associated with sexual energy, creativity.

Third Eye—The Cosmic Eye, or All-Seeing Eye. See Ajna.

Tum-Mo—A Tibetan Buddhist practice which involves developing extraordinary body heat. Tum-Mo is an advanced meditation practice designed to open the energy channels of the body-mind, and infuse the practitioner with power. The ability to generate heat is not the primary aim of Tum-Mo practice. Accomplished Tum-Mo masters can melt and dry as many as a dozen frozen, water-soaked sheets during the course of a single night, with just their body heat.

Visudha—The throat chakra, or energy vortex. Located along the spine near the throat. Associated with creativity and the function of speech.

Will—Sheer determination. Drive and certainty. The ability to neutralize distraction.

Wu-Hsing—The theory of the Five Elements. See Five Elements. Wu-Hsing is the fundamental premise of the *Nei Ching*, also known as the *Yellow Emperor's Classic Of Internal Medicine*, which is the seminal text of Oriental medicine.

Yin and Yang—The Oriental theory of the interplay of polar opposites. Yin is female, night, dark, lunar, and Yang is male, day, light, solar.

Yoga—Union with the Supreme. Yoga is the achievement of Yoga practice. Can also mean any of thousands of systems for attaining such union.

Index

Aboriginal Natives of
  Australia, 17
acupuncture, 34, 119
Ajna, 32, 114, 119
Alexander The Great, 16
Anahata, 31, 114, 119
Anatolev, Alex, 55
anthroposophy, 17
Aura, 35, 48, 119
Aura Builder, The, 47

Balancing Breath, The, 45
Bear Claws, 63
bioenergy, 18
Brahma, 107
Buddha Hands, 55
Buddha Hands Kung Fu, 23,
  40, 89, 119

Cat Stance, 94
Center of the Skull Meditation, 117
Center of the Skull Method,
  117
cerebrospinal fluid, 46, 94, 96,
  119
Chakras, 21, 28, 30, 31, 38,
  51, 53, 78, 84, 94, 97, 99,
  100, 113, 114, 117, 119
Charisma, 31
Chest to Knee Stretching, 64
Chi, 18, 19, 33, 104, 119
Chi Development, 101
Chi Development Method,
  104
Chi Kung, 104, 119
Chuang Fu, 23, 55, 89, 119
clairvoyance, 87, 119
color, 101, 104
color-healing, 102, 119
congruency, 24
cosmic consciousness, 32, 120
Cosmic Meditation, 111

digestion, 95

Ding Le Mei, 44
Double Kicks, 62
dragon, 19, 120
dreams, 100
drugs, 88, 120

ecstacy, 88, 120
Einstein, Albert, 16
ejaculation, 84
Energy Polarization, 23, 101,
  103

Five Elements, 34, 69, 120
Five Elements Exercises, 23,
  35, 71, 120
Five Elements Exercises #1,
  72
  #2, 72
  #3, 74
  #4, 74
  #5, 75
Five Tibetans, 23, 35, 78, 84,
  89, 120
Flying Crane Breathing, 43
Four Noble Truths of
  Buddha, 112

Gandhi, Mohandas K., 16
Goethe, 19
Godlight, 18
Great Yogic Sermon, 19

Hands Together, Elbows to
  Ground, 57
Hara, 104, 120
Hatha Yoga, 87, 120
holding to the truth, 17
Horse Stance, 41, 56, 57

Ida, 30, 33, 45, 90
Immortal Breath, The, 53
immune system, 95
Indra, 107

Initial's Breath, 52
intent, 23
Invincible Breath, The, 49
Invocation of the Shadow,
  The, 23, 107, 108, 109

Karma Yoga, 77, 120
Ki, 18, 19, 33, 120
Knife Defense Stretching, 59
Kundalini, 18, 33, 52, 54, 87,
  88, 89, 91, 92, 95, 99, 100,
  107, 114, 117, 120
Kundalini experiences, 100,
  120
Kundalini Yoga, 23, 28, 30,
  87, 88, 89, 103, 113
Kundalini Yoga Meditation,
  113, 116, 117
Kung Fu, 55, 104, 121

language, 111
Legs Apart, Nose to Floor, 61
Long Deep Breath, The, 39,
  41
Lotus Alternate Knee Breath-
  ing, 93
Lotus Pose, 92, 97, 121
lucid dreaming, 100
magic, 23
Mahadeva, 107
Mahamudra, 95
Manipura, 31, 101, 114, 121
Mantra, 87
Mantra meditation, 111
Maya, 112, 121
meditation, 23, 84, 92, 100,
  111, 112
Meniere's Disease, 115
mental physics, 44
meridians, 21, 34, 121
Microcosmic Orbit, 35, 121
mind altering, 120
Muladhara, 30, 33, 91, 113,
  121
mutual closeness, 69

Creation, 69
destruction, 69
fear, 69

Nad Yoga, 114, 115
Nada, 115, 116, 121
Neck Rolls, 57
Neumann, Therese, 16
Normal Breath, The, 39, 41

Open Lotus Breath, 41
orgasm, 84, 88, 99
Orgone energy, 18
out-of-body experience, 118, 121

Perineum, 30, 121
Pingala, 30, 33, 45, 90
Plexuses, 28
power, 15, 121
Power Breath, The, 45
power generators, 101
Prana, 18, 37, 121
Pranayam, 37, 38, 87, 121
Pratikopasana, 108
Push-Ups on Bear Claws, 63
Push-ups on Palms, 60
Push-ups on Two Knuckles, 67
pygmies, 17

Raja Sundernath, 17
resolution, 20
reverse seal, 96
Rudi, 40

Rudra, 107
Running Buddhas, 18
Sahasrara, 32, 114, 122
satyagraha, 17
sexual abstinence, 84
sexual energy, 31, 84, 96
Shakti, 18, 19, 122
Shakti Breath, The, 54
Siddha, 17, 19, 122
Siddhasan, 91
Silver Cord Meditation, 116
Siva, 107, 108, 116
Siva Samhita, 108
Sixth Tibetan, 84
sleep, 99
Snake Breathing, 42
Solar Plexus, 103
Solar Plexus Chakra, 101
Solar Plexus Charging, 23, 101, 102, 103
Sound Current Meditation, 114, 115
Spinal Twists, 90, 93
Steiner, Rudolf, 17
Stretch #2, 60
Stretching for Side Kick, 66
Stretching for Straight Kick, 65
Sun in the Heart, The, 51
Super Brain Breath, The, 46
Sushumna, 30, 33, 90
Svadhisthana, 30, 113, 122

Tai, 55
Tai Chi, 104
Ten Tibetan Breaths, 23, 44, 88

Tension Release Breath, The, 40
Third Eye, 30, 32, 114
Tibetan Exercises #1, 79
    #2, 80
    #3, 81
    #4, 82
    #5, 83
Tibetan monks, 17
Training Breath, 41
Tribesmen, Kikuyu, 17
Tum-Mo, 17, 101, 122

Vibrational Breath, The, 50
Vigyuna Bhairava Tantra, 98
Visnu, 107
Visudha, 32, 114, 122

Waldorf schools, 17
will, 24, 122
Wisdom Eye, 32
Wu-Hsing, 34, 69, 122

Yang, 30
Yellow Emperor's Classic of Internal Medicine, The, 69
Yin, 30
Yin and Yang, 45, 104, 122
Yoga, 122
Yoga Mudra, 97
Yoganusasanam, 19
Yoganusasanam Bhairava Tantra, 107, 116
Yoni Mudra, 98

zazen, 111